A Place Like Any Other

ALSO BY MOLLY WOLF

Hiding in Plain Sight

A Place Like Any Other

· *Sabbath Blessings* ·

Molly Wolf

Image Books

DOUBLEDAY

New York London Toronto
Sydney Auckland

AN IMAGE BOOK
PUBLISHED BY DOUBLEDAY
a division of Random House, Inc.
1540 Broadway, New York, New York 10036

IMAGE, DOUBLEDAY, and the portrayal of a deer drinking from a stream
are trademarks of Doubleday, a division of Random House, Inc.

Library of Congress Cataloging-in-Publication Data
Wolf, Molly, 1949–
A place like any other : Sabbath blessings / Molly Wolf.— 1st ed.
p.   cm.
"Image books."
1. Meditations. I. Title.
BV4832.2.W64 2000
242—dc21
00-027285

Wolf, Martha Clare [Molly]

September 2000
First Edition
1   3   5   7   9   10   8   6   4   2

Book design by Jennifer Ann Daddio

For Jane, my sister,
who learned in God's good time
how much beauty there is
out there in the wilderness.

Preface

An introduction, of sorts:

I live in an untidy Victorian house much in need of paint and landscaping, in a totally unremarkable beer-and-pretzel-ish small town, in one of the least picturesque areas of a largish Canadian province, and the life I lead is almost completely without interesting incident. I am plain and middle-aged; my hair's usually all over the place, and I could easily lose more than a few pounds. By nobody's standards, much less Martha Stewart's, could my life be considered gracious, orderly, well organized, or even remotely successful. I write. I do a lot of rather ineffectual housework; I deal with my family; I go to church; I try to make some sort of sense of life; I clean up after my cats. Mostly, my life's just a matter of putting one foot after another. As is true for most people, I suppose.

Except. Except.

Except that I find, when I look around, that God keeps intruding, almost always in very small matters. God is lurking behind the scrubby Manitoba maples in the back field and under the

1

long grass down by the creek. God is seeping up like groundwater, in the strangest and sneakiest ways. God is getting creative with the compost pile out back, even while, at the selfsame time, God is also playing hugely and joyously with whole brilliant strands and clusters of wheeling galaxies. God is keeping a loving eye both on the field mice under the wild grape by the stone wall and on my four cats, who are hunting the field mice under the wild grape by the stone wall—and no, I don't understand this obvious contradiction. But then again, God is much, much bigger than anything my tiny mind could conceivably wrap itself around, so of course I can't possibly begin to understand all that God's getting up to, or even a small fraction thereof.

God lies in loving, delighted ambush throughout my days, wanting to wrap and weave around and through my entire life. This is something that (like most people) I have a certain problem accepting, partly because I don't see why God should be so interested and partly because, like most sinners, I have my pride and like my privacy, and there are plenty of bits of me that I would rather that God *not* notice too closely, thank you very much. I know this is a futile endeavor, but I can't help it.

For this reason, I keep trying to find places where God *isn't*, and thus far, I've had no luck. He is indeed "about my paths and my ways," as the psalmist says, and there is no getting away from Him. For God is a lover who wants me, however little I think He should and however often I try to push Him away or hide from Him. In trying to envade Him, or in following lesser and self-appointed gods, I have dug deep down in pits of darkness and spent quite serious time in the desert, but wherever I went, the real God was there before me. He gets around a lot.

When I started writing again, after the best part of twenty-five years' silence, I found myself posting short meditation-type pieces on several Internet mailing lists—and there God was, waiting for me, wanting to be in on the act. So I wrote about finding God in real life. Because I post the pieces on Saturday, they're called "Sabbath Blessings." This book collects a years' worth of these pieces, following the turn of the seasons (we have six hereabouts: fall, mud season, winter, mud season, spring, and summer). I am responsible for the duds in this book. God, and God alone, is responsible for the good stuff.

Many thanks to my agent, the inexpressibly wonderful Linda Roghaar; to my excellent editor at Doubleday, Trace Murphy, and my copy editor, Kacy Tebbel, who caught *all* my typos; to my mother-*cum*-personal theological trainer, Barbara Wolf; and to my menfolk, Henry, Ross, and John, who put up with having a (sometimes very cranky absentminded) writer around the house. Love you, guys.

Part One

Leaf Season

Earthy Stuff

I was all set to write a thoughtful, solemn, intuitive piece about woundedness and grace and all that good stuff, but the weather's been too damned beautiful.

Right now, as I write, the sky is a blue of such depth and intensity as you never see around here except in mid-October, and the sun somehow manages to be a warm kindness without being overly strong. There's just enough chill in the air to make blankets on the bed feel delicious. Of my three huge maples, two are at the exquisite green-gold stage, and the middle one is simply blatant flat-out pure gold with touches of tawny. Its fallen leaves have turned the scruffy side yard by the porch into an emperor's cloak. Those leaves *demand* to be scuffled through, raked into a pile, and jumped in.

This is clearly a week to set down the intellect and pick up the senses—to give Martha a run and let Mary put her feet up. So I walked out to the store through the fine morning, through a field whispering with yellow aspen, touched with the last of the asters, and graced with the annual milkweed miracle. I bought a big round mild yellow onion, bacon, tender beef, carrots, mushrooms, and potatoes, and also a bottle of Merlot, and right now most of those things (except for a tiny glass of Merlot, just a quality check, of course) are becoming intimately acquainted over low heat, smelling wonderful. And for the same reason, three loaves of strong-minded whole-wheat-with-honey bread sit rising in the sun on the picnic table out back. Next on the agenda: cherry pie.

There are times, I believe, when our whole duty to God is to allow ourselves to be happily seduced by creation.

I know this goes contrary to old notions that Material Stuff is Bad and Spiritual Stuff is Good (maybe outdated now, although I suspect that both Gnosticism and Puritanism are alive and well). But: I do not see how it gives glory to God to overcook brussels sprouts, on the grounds that whatever makes you miserable must be good for your soul. True, a certain degree of necessary suffering goes with the honest recognition that we're Miserable Offenders, but I don't see that God intends us to drag the rest of creation through the mud with us. That brussels sprout has not offended, as we have offended; why then should we take our misery out on it by boiling it to death?

It is important, I think, to distinguish between the earthly and the earthy. A Maserati is one sort of thing; beef stew with Merlot is another, especially when the purpose of the stew is to express one's delight in God's creation and one's love for those to be fed. A day spent shopping for three-hundred-dollar Guccis is not the same as a day spent picking apples in the sun. Earthly says, "Make these things your God"; earthy says, "God is here in God's extraordinary creation, give thanks." Earthly says, "We can make and control, and suffer for, and make others suffer for, things we declare to be beautiful and valuable." Earthy invites you to pick up one single fallen leaf from a scarlet maple and be clonked crosseyed by its sheer glory.

It's not often, in the Bible, that God moves center stage, turns to the audience, and speaks directly to us, instead of letting others of us do the talking. But He does exactly that at the end of the Book of Job, saying (in effect), "Okay, bucky, listen up here. I'm going to tell you why I'm God and you aren't." There God is, offered that prize intellectual and theological plum, the Problem of Evil, and if anyone has the solution to that one, God does. God could utter any wisdom in God's unimaginable mind. God could have given us the Unified Field Theory, or the Secret of World Peace, or the Meaning of Life, or whatever. Instead, God gives us a catalogue of creation, from the loosened cords of Orion to the soar of the hawk and the majesty of Leviathan: "Creation I have made, and made beautifully, in ways that delight Me. Can you do the same?"

Creation, this whole week before Thanksgiving, has been singing back to its Creator in a great burst of glory, a huge melodious shout of joy, before it settles down for the quietness of Mud Season and the stillness of Canadian winter. And for a short time it hints at what might lie beyond the River. Will the delights there be all of mind and spirit, not of the "bad" body and senses? I would hate to have God so limited. I feel through the soles of my feet, planted on this warm and vibrant earth, that C. S. Lewis had it right when he wrote at the end of his life:

Then the new earth and sky, the same yet not the same as these, will rise in us as we have risen in Christ. And once again, after who knows what aeons of the silence and the dark, the birds will sing out and the waters flow, and lights and shadows move across the hills and the faces of our friends laugh upon us with amazed recognition.

Guesses, of course, only guesses. If they are not true, something better will be.

(C. S. Lewis, *Prayers: Letters to Malcolm,*
Fount, London, 1977)

Carbon

O kay; that's that," I thought, when I opened the fridge door and got jumped by one lettuce, two tangerines, a container of cherry yogurt, and a pound of hamburger. There's simply too much stuff in there. I'm used to the same phenomenon when I open the freezer door—in fact, I usually step back reflexively, protecting my toes from being dive-bombed by cans of frozen orange juice. But clearly it was time to Do Something about the fridge. So, resolutely, grimly, seriously, I began to unpack its contents.

Oh boy.

Ohboy-ohboy-ohboy.

Hmmmph.

It's really something else, isn't it, what happens to the butt end of an English cucumber after a few weeks, right? Good thing I studied microbiology, the second time I went through university. I could look at the contents of the baggie with a certain detached fascination, but without revulsion. The phrase is "saprophytic growth." After certain microorganisms break down the plant tis-

sues, other microorganisms utilize the released nutrients for growth
... phew! Look at the fungal bloom on that. Wonder how it managed to turn *that* color?

It's called the carbon cycle. A plant soaks up water from the
soil and carbon dioxide from the air and, in its chloroplasts, as-
sembles them into glucose. It glues the glucose together into cellu-
lose to make its own structures, or it uses the glucose directly for
energy. The plant itself inevitably dies, and microorganisms feast
on its stored carbons, converting them into interesting stuff, like
the mess in the baggie. And other organisms feast on the mess, or
on the mess's byproducts, until ultimately it's back to CO_2 and
water again.

The plant also stows some of its glucose in its seed in the form
of starch, for the living germ to use in growth. If the plant is one
of a number of specially bred grasses, we humans harvest the seed
and retrieve the stored starch and add water and yeast and other
stuff, and lo and behold, we have bread. Or maybe it's another spe-
cialized grass that we feed to cattle, whence cometh that pound of
hamburger. Through complex metabolic pathways, we may use
that carbon directly for energy or stow it away in our own flesh,
in muscle or bone or (all too often) fat.

The carbon in lunch—where did it come from? Out of those
billions and billions of carbon atoms in my tuna salad sandwich,
some probably spent some time in another human being. Some
certainly spent time in a dinosaur. But the cycle connects me to *all*
life. I can't be prouder than the guy begging on the street corner,
can't look down on him. We might share atoms from the same
source, after all—just as I might share some atoms with the

microorganisms in the sludge in the baggie. I am in very fact "a part of the whole, a piece of the main."

But sooner or later, inevitably, our own personal carbons return to where they all came from. We yield carbon up daily, or once and for all—in our breath, in our excretions, in the dissolution of our bodies when we die. The psalmist was spot on. But it wasn't dust we came from and return to; it was water and CO_2, plus some other elements like nitrogen and calcium and potassium, each with its own complex cycle through life.

Seems rather pointless? Ah, but what happens along the way? We are our bodies and then some; we grow as people, we interact, we are alive, we love and hate and fear and laugh and mate and (maybe too often?) procreate. We eat and sleep and itch and sing and squabble. We play soccer and grub in our gardens and cuddle our children. We play with kittens, write letters to the editor, lust after strangers. We clean out fridges and hurl insults at each other and comfort those who mourn and exploit each other and do good and evil things. And there are billions of us doing and being and making and becoming, and there are far more billions of other organisms doing and being and making and becoming, and each of us, from rhizopus to emperor penguin, depends on carbon. And hydrogen. And oxygen. And a few other quite basic elements.

It connects us, this elemental cycle. I have unimaginable numbers of carbon atoms stowed away in my own too ample tissues; who knows who owned them before I did? The atoms themselves are highly stable. My personal carbons are billions of years old, and Lord only knows where they've spent all that time. They've been around the block a few million times, that's for sure. And they are mine only temporarily—on loan, as it were.

But while these atoms only belong to me briefly, while they're mine, they are essential to me. They do more than simply carry my immortal soul around; they and it are engaged in a marvelously subtle, intricate, delicate, complex interplay, alternately grave and silly. It's a dance I can only guess at, but my guess is that it's an essential part of my personal soul-making. For what can be more truly ours than our bodies? How else can we live and love and become in this life, but in the flesh? But, at the same time, are our bodies ours at all? For their carbon will return to the air, and our souls to God.

I have it on good authority that it's extremely likely that some of my personal atoms (probably hydrogens—we're more hydrogen than anything else) were once part of the Body that hung on the Cross. But I needn't be vain about this, because that was also true of Adolf Hitler and Joseph Stalin, and while, given their death dates and my birth date, I probably haven't got any of their personal atoms, I probably do have some of Caligula's. This lends a certain strange coherence to the notion of incarnation. We *all* incorporate (literally!) an infinitesimal part of the one who was "incarnate by the Holy Ghost of the Virgin Mary." His flesh is literally part of us. And we are all part of each other, bad guys and good and the in-betweens (which is what most of us are).

One Creator set this cycle in motion. One Creator watches as it cycles, in all its vast interconnectedness—carbons swirling from one creature to another, through the atmosphere, through fossil fuels, through tree trunks and rice and Cheez Whiz and English cucumbers and the bread and wine of the Eucharist. We may draw the boundaries between sacred and secular, but Creator and Creation don't heed them, just as the huge gyre of weather ignores the lines we draw between one country and another. But that gyre may also be profoundly affected by the flap of one butterfly's wings, in ways we cannot begin to imagine.

Such a mass of intricacies and paradoxes and layers and layers of richness and potential meaning that no human mind can reach around and embrace ... What matters? That one Creator, one God, knows and loves each atom of each of His creatures, from bedbug to saint in glory. There is a great grandeur and mystery here.

I carried the bag with the—the—shall we call it a *former* English cucumber?—out to the compost and tilted the contents in on top of the soft, dark, messy, fermenting, mildly odorous, fruit-fly-ridden mass of carbon-in-process, which microorganisms in their gazillions are converting into stuff that adds richness to the soil. It supports a life of its own, this unsightly goop; a bloom of the highly practical, with its own odd beauty. This is time's circle happening here.

And then I put everything worth saving back in the fridge, but more neatly, and closed the door. When I opened the fridge door again, everything stayed where I'd put it. Next time, I think I'll actually wash the shelves.

Raking

Two of my three big maples are almost bare now, and the third—the one out front, my favorite—is letting fly with its last remaining leaves. I love my trees dearly, except for a brief period in late October when I have to clean up after them. It's not a minor matter. They drop enough leaves to fill a small boxcar—far too many to bag, and burning is both illegal and Environmentally Unsound (although I do plan to sneak one small leaf fire, on the grounds that no child should be deprived of the smell of a leaf fire, me included). I don't have a mulcher, and I can't compost this much vegetation. I do fill some garbage bags with leaves and use those to insulate a chilly bit of basement wall, but that still leaves, oh, maybe twenty cubic yards or more. . . . So what we do is rake the leaves into a eight-by-ten-foot tarp, carry them out to my capacious backyard, dump them behind a stone wall, and let Nature take her course.

Older kid and I were out there raking on Wednesday afternoon after school, filing the tarp six times and making a dent in the mess, while the leaves fell as fast as we could rake them. Meanwhile, from across the street came a peculiar whining sound. I finally tracked it down: the lady across the street was vacuuming her yard.

I like this neighbor, a crisp, neat, elderly woman still full of energy. Her yard, on the other hand, dismays me. It is a perfect weed-free emerald-green carpet, meticulously mowed during the summer in perfectly straight lines. She has a tidy little garden too, to go with her honest foursquare little white house. I imagine that everything inside is clean and orderly, the carpets vacuumed regularly, windows cleaned twice a year, bathrooms sparkling. I imagine she's the sort of person who always balances her checkbook and keeps proper household accounts.

I, on the other hand, have a shambling Victorian mess of a house, seriously in need of cleaning and painting and rotting in spots. A piece of the eavestroughs fell off a couple of years ago and is still hanging around on the side porch. Indoors is partly reasonably organized chaos and partly unorganized chaos. The household bills, once paid, go into a large cardboard box, which I will sort out when I can find the time. I couldn't balance a checkbook if you paid me, and the whole idea leaves me vaguely uneasy, like the smell of something dead in the garage. If the kids and I work very hard, we can get rid of the bulk of the leaves, but there's no way we can get the yard CLEAN. This gives me a serious case of the guilts, which I can never quite put down. Dammit, I should be able to manage better . . .

But on Wednesday, under a dark blue sky with the leaves drifting gold onto the patch of grass I'd just barely cleared, I stood for a few moments, leaning on my rake, and reality broke in like the dawn. My neighbor, bless her, is retired, lives alone, and has a great deal of time. I am a single parent trying to run a large house singlehanded, in spite of my kids, while earning a living the hard way as a contract writer. My neighbor has one tidy little maple tree that hasn't really turned yet. I have three huge trees that have just dumped their very considerable contents over a comparatively small space. Her little leaf blower would be hopelessly inadequate to deal with this mess. Not only that, I realized, but this isn't me making excuses (as my guilt-mongering conscience claims). This is reality. This is *true*.

Why do we judge ourselves and each other so ruthlessly, without ever considering our own or the others' circumstances? We look sideways at each other, comparing notes and feeling righteously indignant, or hopelessly inferior, or smugly judgmental, or totally inadequate. We're quick to assume the worst and slow to count the best. And we drag God into it, assuming that God wants to do the same.

But what if God refuses to make comparisons? What if God looks at Mother Teresa and says, "Wonderful job; I love you very much" and ALSO says to the no-good *nebbish* propping up the bar down at the hotel, "I know why you fetched up like this; I love you very much"? What if God, looking at my good and tidy neighbor, says, "Thank you for creating such a beautiful lawn and keeping it so neat" AND says to me, "Thank you for enjoying My trees, and what's a few unswept leaves between friends"? What if God insists on seeing what it is—however little!—that we do what's good right and loving and proper, while being perfectly willing to understand why, sometimes, we screw up or fail so badly? What if God *knows* just what it is that jars the arm so that the shot misses the mark? We are all, compared to God, so small, so frail, so less than good, so very badly wounded. God knows that.

Who says that God's logic is like ours? Our justice says "tit for tat" and "don't make excuses" and "you should have tried harder"— but is that God's justice? Maybe God's justice is to ours as chaos theory is to Pythagorean geometry: that is, God's justice *contains* our "justice," but our justice is only a small, primitive part of His justice. Maybe that's why Jesus tells us over and over, in the strongest possible language, not to judge others: because Jesus, unlike the rest of us, knew what God's justice truly is. And knowing God's notion of justice and how poorly our notion of justice approaches God's, he warns us strongly: "Do not, under any circumstances, try this at home."

Maybe, in hanging around with loose-living Samaritan women at wells and with lowlife types and scabrous lepers and the like, Jesus was saying something about God's justice as well as God's love. Maybe God *sees* something in irresponsible welfare mothers and drug dealers and people who don't try as hard as we think they should. Maybe God sees things in the frivolous exploitative unthinking rich that I don't see. Maybe God's justice holds these people in the palm of God's hand, tenderly retracing the track of their lives, seeing the wounds that sent them spinning off course, and grieving for the deep and early harm that causes them to hurt themselves and others. Yes, we have trouble with that sort of justice; but then, we are creatures of such limited empathy, such tiny imagination.

As these thoughts twirled in my mind like the leaves through the air, I found I could look both at my neighbor's beautiful emerald carpet and my own messy yard and feel—not that my yard isn't a mess, something I'm responsible for and have to manage as best I can—but that I really *can't* do it all. Honestly and honorably, the Lawn Beautiful is beyond my best capacity. If that's okay by God, I guess I have to go along. If God can forgive me for being a much less than perfect person—for being messed up and inadequate and incapable of keeping up with the workload—then I guess I'll have to forgive me too.

Back to raking. I'll do what I can, God. That's all I can promise. It will have to do.

Nice Gods

Normally it's not hard to soothe Pete down. He does flap sometimes, and gets into gently anxious states, but we talk stuff through and he usually regains his balance quickly enough.

The other day was different. It had been a bad week—a worse week than he'd acknowledged even to himself, much less to his friends—and he was REALLY tense and edgy and almost snappish (by Pete standards, which are not exactly snappish by normal standards). Normal friend-type soothing wasn't making a dent in it, either. Not that he was being a Big Problem; Pete never is. He's a gentle guy and the best of company. Merely he was strung tight, and I couldn't help but be aware of it. It showed in his voice and the set of his shoulders, and in an unwonted inner perturbed remoteness that isn't, for him, a healthy way to be.

We tend to see sin in terms of Bad Behavior or in great philosophical abstractions—or, more sneakily, in others' presumptuousness in being Different from our own preciously right selves. But we don't tend to see sin as a state of being badly out of sorts. And yet for most of us who do not commit Horrible Acts and are good Christians in thought and deed, that sort of edginess, vague disquiet, inner tension, may be the thing we need saving from worst.

I could trace Pete's state back to one of the Seven Deadlies— Envy, in this case. He is not the person he thinks he should be; he feels that he should be X when God made him Y, because he hasn't yet accepted that there's nothing wrong with being Y. But you can get into very much the same state of being through any of the others—Covetousness, Lust, Anger, Sloth, Gluttony, or that granddaddy of them all, self-regarding, self-centered Pride.

Maybe we should drop the word "sin" altogether. Sin, in the conventional sense, had nothing to do with Pete. So far from behaving badly, he was gently apologetic for being less than his usual beamish self. Nor does the word apply as used in its theological sense. Pete hadn't turned his back on God and stomped off. Not in the least.

And yet this inner sense of wrong *felt* like something he needed to be redeemed from. If I had to diagnose, I'd say that Pete had enthroned this ideal X in God's place, but Pete's ideal X cannot love Pete as God can love Pete. In fact, there's no way Pete can ever live up to X's expectations and X is not even slightly forgiving. Pete's state of low-grade misery was the result of being deprived of God's love because he was looking to the wrong god.

We establish ideals of (for example) being independent and self-sufficient, and we set these up as gods and then feel desolate when they fail to be adequately loving gods. Or we worship materialism and feel bleakly empty when it doesn't fill the emptiness in us. Or we have something (or someone) perfect in mind and are haunted by our inability to find and keep it (him/her/them). Or we have some state we'd like to get to—I'll be happy when I get this, or weigh that, or earn this much, or meet that person.

We are mostly good people, well-behaved people, mannerly and law-abiding people who don't seriously bend the Commandments. Still, we go around with that sense of hollowness that comes from having something empty that should be filled with real love. But we do not want to ask for, or accept, real love. In fact, we may fend it off as fast as we can. Because Love insists on seeing us as the needy, incomplete, lonely people we are, not as the good, happy, all-together people we think we are, or would like to be.

Pete was lucky; he got miserable enough in the end to let down his hair and admit that he *was* miserable, and to accept a little comfort and reassurance. Many people don't reach that point. They don't look for salvation because they've misdefined what it is that (mostly) we need saving from. Oh, sure, some of us need saving from Big Bad Ugly things, like drugs or alcohol, abuse or the horrors of war, grave illness or great sorrow. Some of us are genuine Bad People who do horrible things and need that sort and level of forgiveness.

But more often than not we need to be saved from that gnawing sense that Something's Wrong: there's a grief in the room somewhere, but nothing you could put your finger on. And that sense is an inner signal that we may have put something in God's place that is not God, and cannot love as God loves.

It's so hard to accept, God's love, because God expects us to say "I really do need you." And why are those words so very hard to say?

Gravity Is With Us on This Side of the Hill

(TO JOHN, WITH LOVE)

I'm not sure whether it's because he's getting bigger or because I'm getting weaker, but I find I can no longer carry my younger kid up the stairs to bed. We found this out the other night. As usual, after he'd had brushed his teeth and got into his PJs, we curled up on the blue sofa, under the throw, and listened to the Songs We Always Listen to Before John Goes to Bed. Halfway through the third one, I realized that his gorgeous long lashes were down on a cheek fast losing its baby roundness. He was out like a light. I tried to hoist him up to bed, but three steps up the back stairs, I had to set him down, and he staggered the rest of the way under his own steam, much put out and protesting sleepily.

I'd had intimations of mortality a few days before, when I tried to lug ninety pounds of water-softener salt from the car to the house and simply could not do it. No way, José. The salt entered my house in installments. This is frustrating; I used to be extremely strong, and proud of it, just as I used to be proud of my emotional toughness. I used to be able to lug a hundred pounds up a flight of stairs or put up with a faceful of abuse without blinking, and now I'm starting to lose it. Rats.

Or so I thought, until I considered the people I want to be like when I grow up, if I ever do, and realized that they're all exceedingly gentle people. I don't mean weak—they aren't wusses by any means. In fact, looking around the group, I see that they are all extremely strong people whose strength has softened with time and experience. And in that gentleness lies much of my delight in their company.

When we're young, we tend to see softness as weakness; we expect body and soul alike to be strong, courageous, muscular, agile, self-confident. We expect our souls, like our legs, to carry on tirelessly, leaping from crag to crag, climbing the peaks, racing down to the valleys. Then we take a few tumbles, fall off a cliff or two, break a few bones, spend some time sitting and convalescing and doing some serious thinking, losing a little muscle tone . . . and then we find that we've lost some of our strength and much of our scrappiness.

Learning to love means giving up and taking on; and one of the giving-ups is the giving up of much righteousness and clarity and strong-mindedness and other youthful strengths. In fact, it worries me when I see someone over "a certain age" who's still absolutely sure of The Facts and ready to brawl, because I suspect a certain rigidity has set in, instead of the mellowing and ripening that we go through, given God's grace and a few good solid whomps upside the head.

"Taking on" means taking on some qualities that, when we're young, seem shameful. The ability, for example, to admit that we've been wrong—not that we've made an eentsy little booboo, but that we've really seriously blown it, done real harm and genuine wrong, and must ask pardon of God and our fellows, argh! That's very hard to swallow. So is the realization that pain isn't to be heroically carried around at arm's length, but taken deep into one's soul and used for purposes of maturation—ouch! So often stoicism is simply the refusal to take pain properly to heart; I speak as one who knows. . . . And then there's humility, sometimes a very bitter pill indeed; beginning to realize the extent to which we've put ourselves at the center of the universe, had our vision warped by self-centeredness, misinterpreted others' signals through our own oversensitivity, acted as though we were the only ones around. We must eat our own Shadows, our darker sides—first recognizing them as a true and important part of our selves, and then accepting them genuinely and with humility. It can be rough going.

But there are gains. I may be less strong in body than I once was, but I find I'm less clumsy and impetuous when I move with the new deliberation of middle age—less apt to knock things over or step where I shouldn't. I see my own darker side, but that allows me to accept its reality, to see some of its benefits, and to keep it in better check. Accepting my own failings helps me to be a little more charitable about others'. I think I am more patient than I once was.

If we lose agility, we may have gained something in wisdom. If we lose speed, we've perhaps improved out in-depth observation, our perseverance, our endurance, our sense of inner peace. If we lose the zest for battle, we gain serenity and a new balance. If we lose our old swift certainty and clarity of vision, perhaps we gain a delighted appreciation of the beauty of shadow and paradox. The colors may be less clear and bright than they once were, but they are far richer.

I used to like a good fight, and I can still fight when I need to, but it's no fun any more. I want a true peace with those around me—not an armed truce, but the sort of peace in which all lay their armor down, knowing it will not be needed, because we will study war no more. I want to sit quietly with others in charity and kindness and the silent happiness of being together in undemanding, accepting love. If others want to fight, there are plenty of people who still enjoy that; it's not my pleasure any more—I'd sooner sing.

In this latter half of my life I have every intention of getting softer, not harder, by the day. And if that means getting weaker in body, well, that's a fair price to pay, and I'll pay it happily. After all, Jesus said we were to become like little children; and besides, this way, I may not have to shovel the driveway forever.

Fortunately, my kids are growing stronger; it won't be long before their strength passes mine. It's their turn to have strong, hard, active young bodies and the strength and agility of belief that go with it. *They* can carry the water-softener salt in from the car and see things in glorious clear-cut black and white. For me, I plan to work on getting milder, not harder; more pliant, not stronger; gentler, not more courageous. Like butcher's beef, I intend to age into tenderness.

And the soul I will take into the Life to Come won't, I hope, be tough at all.

Push-Pull

Black cat Dynamite jumped up beside me on the sofa a while ago, demanding a fuss. He settled himself comfortably in the crook of my arm, allowing himself to go completely limp while I scratched industriously away, finding the itchy spots around his glossy head and neck. And then, when his trust grew to boldness, he rolled over like a baby, kneading the air with his paws, stretching his elegant neck back and sticking out an absurd fringe of pink tongue, purring ecstatically while I scratched his hard little belly.

Then a truck backfired outside, and Dyna-cat shot off as though he'd been scalded.

That's Dynamite: 90 percent total paranoia, 10 percent total trust. He came to us as a terrified half-grown kitten, allowed by the other cats to join our household. My guess is that he'd been somebody's pet until he started turning from cute kitten into real cat, or until he became inconvenient, and then his owners dumped him in the country "where someone would be bound to take him in." Happens all the time out here. Clearly he was seriously traumatized, and he's never quite gotten over it, even after four years of love and safety and unlimited kibble. He is still given to panic attacks, bolting for cover when a door slams and leaving exit wounds (the wounds left when a cat exits) if you try to grab him. But when he does trust, he trusts with his whole feline soul and beautiful coal-black body, a total surrender.

Are we so very different? I think of friend A, who alternates between a gentle care for others and a gentle selfishness; or B, who presents great strength on the surface and is actually easily intimidated; or C, who alternates between anxious obsessiveness and a deeply serene quiet courage; or D, who is genuinely loving but still radiates great anger; or E, who seems tough as nails and is keeping a soft and gentle self firmly concealed from public view; or F, who varies from tremendous energy and efficiency to schlumpish sloth. We are ourselves and our own opposites, X and –X, and we flap helplessly between one and the other, confusing ourselves and those who have to deal with us.

We are pulled two ways: toward Love and Light and wholeness and healing, but also toward the Dark—toward quick fixes and easy answers, toward bad habits and the Seven Deadlies (Pride, Sloth, and Anger being particularly fetching). One writer I just read talks about our being pulled between Eros and Thanatos, life and death. And it seems that becoming more aware, more mature, only deepens and darkens the struggle, as we become simultaneously more and more aware of God's grace—and of how badly we need it.

Maybe part of our becoming-process as souls is to learn to accept this push-pull as normal and natural. It's not that we should give in to Thanatos, but we must become aware that we are, after all, merely human creatures with our dark as well as bright sides. We're not really okay, and no matter what we do, how hard we work at transcending our Thanatos, we are incorrigibly *human*. Always the Darkness calls as well as the Light, and while we must move toward the Light, we're going to hear the call of the Dark— we can't help it, any more than Dynamite can help being paranoid. That's our humanity, our nature. It's itchy knowledge, uncomfortable and edgy-making, but it's necessary. Accepting that Thanatos is an innate part of ourselves is a terribly difficult business. We'd as soon be deaf to our own darker urgings, blind to our own counterproductive patterns, dumb about our own neuroses.

But if being so merely human is such an awful thing, something for which we think we should be punished, then why did God choose to put this skin on Himself? He didn't have to, after all, any more than he had to die. But he chose to be one of us, subject to the same forces that drag us hither and yon. I don't doubt that Jesus too could hear the call of the Darkness—he heard it in the desert, in the Garden, and on the Cross. He too knows how strong the call can be, what it takes to keep moving toward the Light. He didn't act on temptation, but he felt the tug of it, Paul tells us. And when Peter gave in to his own inner Dark and flew off terrified, betraying, giving in to Thanatos completely—Jesus could see Peter with clear but unbent love.

Don't you think God gives us credit, knowing how hard it can be? Maybe that's what mercy and forgiveness are about: Jesus knowing, from the inside, what each of us struggles with—what inner voices call us in ways that we know are wrong but that we cannot always resist. Knowing, he loves us the more for our struggle and our sometimes failures, just as I love Dyna-cat for his fear as well as his occasional whole-body trust.

It's okay for Dynamite to be so full of fear; I can imagine where it comes from, and it just makes me fonder of him—it makes his trust more beautiful by contrast. I have to accept that, just possibly, God is fully aware of how very human I am, full of my own fears and slothfulness and pride and selfishness, and that God chooses to love me and accepts my humanity, knowing that I struggle with it. And I'm starting to wonder if maybe most of us aren't like this. I don't know about everyone; maybe someone out there has thanatos wrestled to the mat, has got it all together, has reached "that peace which passes understanding." I'm not there myself, but I'm beginning to imagine that maybe, just maybe, God will forgive me for being where I cannot help being.

Humanity, humility, humane: all related, all rooted in humus, the dirt. We have to push our roots into it while still growing up toward the Light.

Dynamite just jumped up on the chair beside me, nudging me with his cold nose until I lifted my elbow and let him tuck himself in his favorite position. I'm typing now with a high-gloss coal-black cat wedged between my arm and body, leaning up hard against me. He's purring rapturously, closing his yellow eyes. In a moment, something will happen to terrify him and he'll be gone again; but for now, just for a moment, he seems to be at peace with himself, with me, and with the world.

Thalking

We've invented a portmanteau word "thalk" to describe the process of reaching a decision by talking it out at the kitchen table. ("Thalk" = "think" + "talk"). The talk part is important because you need another person to give you feedback, to keep you balanced, to correct you when you're being unreasonable, to send you spinning off in new and promising directions, and to give you positive feedback when you're on track.

Friend Susan was over this morning thalking through some difficult aspects of her relationship with her beloved Charles. It's tough for Susan because she's still recovering from seventeen years of marriage to an abusive fruitcake—her ex-husband Mike's psyche is fascinating, the way the underside of a rotting log can be fascinating. Charles isn't exactly a piece of cake as a partner, but he's a huge improvement.

But we get conditioned to respond in certain ways, and part of the healing process is to become aware of those ways and patiently undo them—often going back to their beginnings and consciously working through better alternative ways of reacting. So Susan has to sort through her reactions quite carefully, distinguishing what's reasonable from what's a carryover from the past. That's where the thalking process comes in useful.

It would be infinitely simpler for Susan if she just assumed that Mike and Charles are really much of a muchness—set up some rigorous rules and followed them, regardless of the real differences between now and then. And, unfairly, this is what some women do—assume that All Guys Are Jerks and the heck with it. But Susan *does* see a real difference between Mike and Charles. What's sauce for the one isn't sauce for the other. This isn't a place for simple black-and-white logic.

In fact—and this is what makes life peculiarly Interesting and difficult—sometimes the very things that she should NOT have done with Mike, she should be doing with Charles. Sometimes she has to act in ways that were, in the past, terribly damaging, but which are now exactly what she should be doing. Other times, her behavior really does need to change. And it's all small stuff that needs an awful lot of thalking through (which is good for me too, since we're dealing ofttimes with the very same issues).

It's called discernment, and it is a detailed, difficult, painstaking process. Susan has to weigh what is apparently best for her with what is apparently best for Charles and what is apparently best for the relationship—and the three can seem distressingly different. She has to thalk through very strong emotional reactions that are carryovers from the painful past, but that are now inappropriate, given this very different present. She *did* follow simple straightforward rules of Good Christian Behavior in her dealings with Mike, and those rules betrayed her miserably. That, too, needs to be sorted out. So our thalks are wide-ranging and in depth and usually need at least three mugs of tea.

Eventually, she sorts out the strands and figures out what she should be doing. Sometimes she decides that the Problem (whatever it is) is hers, and it's up to her to solve it. Sometimes she decides that it's Charles's, and she needs to confront the guy and ask him to Do Something about it. And sometimes it's something about the way they're operating, which they have to work through together. Or sometimes, after enough thalking, the problem spontaneously disappears. I just help with the initial sorting out; I don't prescribe, any more than she prescribes for me.

Black-and-white solutions are so very much simpler. And they do have some advantages. Susan can operate in this difficult painstaking way with Charles, but she couldn't invest this sort of energy in her relationship with (say) her boss or her kid's teacher—there's only so much room for discernment in a life, given how time- and energy-consuming the process can be.

In some ways, life would be so much easier if we could keep it all straight and narrow. Always do this; never do that. Follow the rules to the letter and you'll be safe. Don't step outside the boundaries. All sex outside marriage is wrong. All members of group X are like this; all members of group Y are like that. It's all in the Bible. Always forgive. Never change. Stick to the doctrine. Don't question. There are no exceptions.

But why, in practice, does this never seem to work out as we'd expected? Why, so many times, do these rules betray us in real life?

Why can they be so obviously cruel or silly in human terms? Why does this process of discernment matter so much, difficult and time-consuming as it is?

Because it's a funny thing, but black-and-white isn't the color of flesh. Or, for that matter, of love.

Small Spider

L ord only knows where the tiny spider came from, but somehow it had fetched up in my front hair. Now it was happily
spinning its way down past my left eye, finding a temporary berth
just to the side of my nose. It tickled. Very distracting, when you're
trying to read. . . .

I freed myself by lifting its silk away from my face, and held
the little thing out, watching it scoot up its invisible but oh so
sturdy line to my fingertip, and rappel back down, looking for an
attachment point for web-building purposes. I draped the silk over
the knob of the pantry door, next to my chair, where (once it
started to spin again) I could watch the spider slide down its invisible line and scuttle back up. I like spiders, and this was a pretty
one: a soft mouse-brown, neatly proportioned, its delicately
banded legs so tiny they were transparent.

I wondered if, when spinning its way down from my hair, it
could see my face. Probably not. It would be like trying to see the
face of a mountain while you're rappelling down the side of it. My

middle-aged mug would be unimaginably *large* to this minute creature, my nose the length of a city block to it, the pores like good-
sized potholes. My face would be mere ground to it, a solid
surface, warmer than most; but incomprehensible. If I moved my
head, would it be able to tell? Probably not, any more than I can
tell the swing of this ball of Earth around the sun.

What can a spider see, anyway? I don't know much about spider vision; I do know that scorpions have even more eyes (twenty-
some; spiders have eight) but are functionally blind and "see" with
their feet. Even if spiders see better than scorpions, I doubt if they
have color vision; and of course their visual centers aren't going to
be sophisticated, by mammalian standards at least. So I don't know
what that little thing could have taken in about my face, except
that it probably wasn't a whole lot. That spider's view of me would
necessarily be partial and incomplete, and very likely just plain
wrong. At least by our standards. . . .

It would be easy for the spider to take in small parts of Hair,
Forehead, Left Eyebrow, Left Eye, and Left Side of Nose while entirely missing Right Eyebrow, Right Eye, Right Side of Nose,
Mouth, both Cheeks, and Chin, not to mention everything else
about me. The spider's view, let's face it, is seriously incomplete.
Not that this is a deficiency on the spider's part: it's partly the spider's own quite normal, natural limitations and partly the sheer
difference in size.

And then I thought: The spider in my face is like me in the
face of God. I can take in so very little, and so much of what I
can take in is just plain wrong—not anyone's fault, just my own
limitations as a being, and the sheer difference in size. God is to

me, not as I am to the spider, but as the spider is to the Earth. Or the universe. Or God, for that matter. God is simply unimaginably *large* and different in ways I cannot begin to imagine.

And yet so close . . . Maybe if God sometimes seems far away or remote, it's simply because we cannot possibly take in the immediacy of God, the hugeness of God so up-close to us that we can't even begin to see it in its immensity—any more than the spider could see me. We go about our lives before the face of God, without even realizing that it *is* God's face, because God's face is so big that we can't really see it, and so familiar that we treat it as part of the landscape. God as wallpaper . . .

But God is infinitely *un*familiar too. God's face is so completely foreign to what we know of life that we can't begin to take it in. God's face is not only huge to us; it blazes with a love that we cannot even begin to apprehend—whole leaping, flaring, fiery sunspots of love, arching in deepest longing toward us, aching for us, begging us to respond, asking us to just *look* as best we can, and forgiving us for the littleness of the look we can give back in love.

And still that's all wrong, wrong, wrong. I'm only getting the tiniest impression of maybe a microfraction of one atom of God's left eyebrow (if God has eyebrows?) because God's love is also as cool and calm, as refreshing and fragrant as quiet flowering woodlands in moonlight after the softest of rains: God comes "all so still" to wherever we are, with such gentleness and such depth of understanding.

Or as the sea, toppling mountains.

God is further from me than the whole known universe is

from that spider, and at one and the same time, God is far nearer to me than my own skin. I know infinitely less of God than the spider did of the side of my nose. But God knows every atom of me, from that atom's origins in the furthest reaches of time to its final fate, whatever awaits at the end.

As God knows this spider . . . who, after I moved it, curled up briefly, probably feeling defensive (or the spiderly equivalent). Then, swiftly adapting to its new location, it swung a purposeful line from the cupboard doorknob to the toaster. Doing what its nature told it, it started to build, spinning industriously, neatly, competently (is there such a thing as an incompetent spider?)—as though it knew the whole meaning and purpose of life.

And on its own terms, perhaps it did. At least, enough for this spiderly life that lies before it.

Part Two

Mud Season (1)

A Place Like Any Other

The maple leaves are down, back behind the old cemetery, a great drift of them. They're a bit damp from the recent rains and so are less satisfactorily crackly than they were, but still, it's a bounden duty at this season.... So on my way back from the grocery store with a backpack full of cherry yogurt, eggs, and oranges, I scuffled/shuffled through them, doing a thorough job of it. One must, after all.

I've known these trees for most of thirteen years now. Like the trees along my street and my house's own particular trees, they are part of the landscape I live with. It's not a particularly handsome landscape; it's a little scruffy, a little unfocused, mildly apologetic. There's nothing special about it except for the river to the north, flowing broad and silver and placidly powerful. Other than that, it's just . . . a place.

Right now, as the last of the leaves subside and we settle once again into Mud Season, it all looks drab and a little seedy. You could drive past the town where I live without a second thought on your way from Ottawa to (say) New York, with no notion of who or what lives here—what small dramas are enacted, who is suffering or happy. You could be comfortably cocooned in your car on the main road, listening to music, sipping good coffee, glancing at the exit signs as they flew past you. And the place would evade you utterly.

And yet: I know for myself that I could not write or make my own soul if I weren't rooted here—or at least rooted somewhere. It's as though I have to kick against the Earth to get anywhere near Heaven or Hell. We tend to think of Good and Evil on the grand scale, of salvation and damnation in broad operatic terms, but really, it all happens here—in a flock of pigeons bursting upward over the old always-for-sale-no-takers ex-hotel, in grubby apartments over failed stores on the main drag, at the truck center and the beer store. God's souls are the worn-out overweight women in unbecoming jogging suits in the workaday supermarket and the paunchy middle-aged guys in their Chevy trucks down by the greasy spoon. They are the louche teenagers skateboarding down by the discount clothing place, the closed-faced children biking back from the playground.

We're all God's souls, scruffy as we are—but don't romanticize us. We aren't all good people, the salt of the earth. We can be stupid and selfish and as unappealing in soul as we are in body. But we are all God's nonetheless.

Gloss, smoothness, fresh paint are all so much more attractive. We think we owe it to ourselves, given our stressed-out lives, to live friction-free, to take it easy, have it predictable—no nasty surprises. We give up rootedness for sleekness, the roadhouse (where the pie is really good) for the safe speed of McDonald's, where no one will invade our privacy and no two hamburgers vary by a millimeter from state to state and year to year. We live in cookie-stamp houses with beautiful finishes. We don't mend our clothes (who has time?); we throw them out. We shop in polished malls, safe from the weather and the street poor, soothed by creamy, attentive materialism. We eat whatever the latest fad is, radicchio or raspberry salsa. We turn our backs on myth and history. And then we wonder why it is we never feel at home.

But home isn't necessarily a neat and tidy place, physically or emotionally. Home's all in the friction. We do much of our best soul-work by rubbing up against each other's roughnesses, banging into elbows, getting necessarily rattled. Spiritual growth can be exhilarating and joyous, but it can also be confusing and exhausting, shaky-making, fractious—even enraging.

Love's not in grandeur and holy heroism; it's in the dailiness of things, in the slightly agonizing give-and-take of trying to do the best we can by each other. I need this; you need the opposite. If I put my need aside for yours, am I doing the most loving thing I can by both of us? Or am I just choosing the easy route? If you demand an apology and I think I've done nothing wrong, should I say, "I'm sorry"? It's almost dismaying, how completely *ordinary* this work is; there is nothing special or grand about it, any more than there's anything special or grand about this place.

But who said that God isn't deeply here in the ordinary, living with us where we are? I keep coming back to this place I live, not for its specialness and beauty, but for the lesson it teaches: that God's beauty is not our beauty. God's beauty may, in fact, be wrapped snug in a ratty old towel and laid in a lost shopping cart in the desolate empty lot back behind the old Canadian Tire store. God's work in us may not involve huge noble sacrifices that secretly scratch our need to feel pleasantly heroic. It may or may not involve forms of beauty that please us, or disciplines that require us to bear suffering nobly. It may only be suppressing a snap when a child wants attention, making a small choice here, putting aside a desire there, being cheerful when we'd rather not be, speaking honestly when that's difficult, getting up an hour early, setting aside a worry in order to listen attentively. God's pleasures may lie as much in the noise of two tired feet scuffling through a drift of maple leaves as in the greatest and highest work of art or charity.

God is here. All we have to do is to notice, to be aware of it, and God's love washes through and over the ordinariness like a sideways light, glinting on the pigeons' wings, flooding the ordinary leaf-littered grass and turning it to subtle gold and soft umber. And then it becomes so easy to love this plainness, to see the beauty that shines softly through this shabbiness—a beauty that seems strangely more immediate in empty lots than in shopping malls, however tastefully decorated.

The faces of the worn-out women in the market are soft and ready to smile back when you smile at them, and their rounded bodies are gently powerful. You notice one of the paunchy good ol' boys buying flowers for his woman, with a secret soft smile that he doesn't even know about, and suddenly you can look past his failures and failings; for a moment, he's twenty again and handsome as a prince. You trade a friendly word with an elderly woman walking her very elderly dog, united in companionable kindness. You hear the skateboarding kids shout out the intense delight of the young in their own youth and quick skill. The kids do wheelies on their bikes, and joy spins out shining from their bike wheels like flying gravel. And the sun comes out and lights the leaves in glory.

All very ordinary. Full of friction. Nothing special. Just a place like any other.

Need Metanoia!

The tooth—it was an upper-right molar—began to mutter at me on Wednesday night, but I chose to ignore it. There's a work crunch on, and I really couldn't take time off for the dentist; and besides, I have a dental appointment next Tuesday. Surely I could stick it out. By Thursday late afternoon, the tooth was no longer muttering; it was singing gently but plaintively, a little humming singsong of Toothache. By Friday morning the song had gone from a pianissimo to a mezzo piano. Clearly waiting till Tuesday was no longer an option. So I stole an hour from work and got the tooth looked after.

Interesting stuff, pain. I can remember once getting a viral neuralgia (I think it was?) with brief episodes of pain so intense that it stopped me in my tracks; for those ten or fifteen seconds, I literally could not move. Likewise, I broke and dislocated a thumb once, and I remember the pain as being so intense that it made me feel faint. And, of course, I have birthed two babies. . . .

Which got me thinking, as I ate soft things for lunch and

nursed my poor bedeviled tooth, that it's wrong to think of pain as being a unitary sort of thing. We tend to see pain as a Good Thing, to be embraced by martyrdom (however teased and invited) because Suffering Strengthens the Character. Or we tend to see pain as a Bad Thing, something to avoid at all costs, because, dammit, it *hurts.*

But my tooth pain, like my thumb pain years ago, was neither good nor bad; it was a necessary warning signal: Body saying to Brain, THIS PROBLEM HAS TO BE FIXED *RIGHT NOW,* NO KIDDING, HOP TO IT!!! Some pain stems from pathology—in fact, the inability to feel this pain *is* pathological. Ignoring that signal isn't stoicism but stupidity. The viral pain, on the other hand, was just one of those things to be endured as best I could. It wasn't something I felt I needed help with; I just waited it out. It was purely incidental pain—not a signal to do something, but simply pain that happened in the nature of things. And of course the pain of childbirth does accomplish something: a baby. That pain is productive. Major difference.

Then it occurred to me that it's possible to transfer all this to the psychospiritual realm, quite neatly. We tend either to wallow in psychospiritual agony, rolling happily in our own sinfulness and grabbing aholt of the Pain of the Whole World (without, of course, wondering if the whole world has asked us to do this, which it usually hasn't). We do this because we think that psychospiritual agony is a Good Thing and proves what Good People and Noble Suffering Souls we are. Or we try to avoid psychospiritual pain altogether. I can't remember: was it Jung or Freud who said, "Neurosis is almost always an attempt to avoid legitimate suffering"? Problem is, we usually make those around us do our suffering for us. . . . Or, combining the two (most interesting!) we may wallow in our Miserable Offenderhood as a way of ducking out on doing our own legitimate suffering, because then we can claim to have Paid Our Dues and can't be expected to suffer further. Huh.

Like my tooth, some of our pain of heart or soul or spirit may indicate a pathology. It may be a signal that there's something we really do need to do something about, the pain of legitimate existential anguish. It's the wise subconscious saying "Need to change!" the way my tooth was saying "Need dentist!" Ignoring that pain, expecting it to go away (as I hoped my tooth pain would) is stupid, although, to be fair, sometimes a person can't immediately act in the necessary ways, just as the poor may not be able to afford dentistry. Metanoia needs its kairos; which, being translated from theology-speak, means: we need a change in direction (metanoia), but sometimes it has to come in God's good time (kairos).

Probably most emotional pain, on the other hand, is merely incidental to living in this world, and there's not a fool thing you can do but endure and make of it the best you can. Learning to live with other people means living with their pointy elbows and toes, and it requires us to develop a reasonably tough hide and a decent level of stoicism. Sometimes we are required to live with the natural consequences of nature itself, which can be extremely painful, as when someone beloved dies. The important thing is to make something of this pain, to let it teach us our humanity, our limits—including the limits of stoicism!

And some pain is productive: the pain of real compassion, the pain of setting the beloved free when we want to cling, the pain of being patient and trusting God, the pain of letting go of the past and moving on, the pain of learning to love and love truly, the pain of accepting our own mortality, the pain of becoming truly aware of ourselves and others, the pain that goes with growth and healing and learning. This is the pain that comes from living life to its deepest and fullest extent, without reservation or hesitation. And it helps to make our souls. It's this sort of pain that we're called upon as Christians to take on with full acceptance.

So: which is which?

The obvious answer: it depends where the pain is coming from and where it's tending to go. Does the pain come from a problem that has to be dealt with? Is it coming from a sick situation and tending in ways that damage the soul? Then take steps to deal with whatever's causing it. Is it just one of those things, like whanging your thumb with a hammer? I think it's legitimate to swear and cuss and weep and run cold water over the afflicted joint—and learn to hammer more accurately, if that's an option. Sometimes life is just Like That. People do die. Accidents do happen. We grieve, and get on.

But productive pain—that you go at willingly, because it is the other side of joy. Christ died that we might live; he suffered in love for us, not for the sake of suffering. He suffered for God's purposes, not Pilate's. His suffering came from love and led to rebirth; it tended toward God's glory. Christ's pain on the Cross was the ultimate productive pain. It was not the pain of pathology, for surely no person in human history was as robustly healthy as Jesus. No need for metanoia there. Nor was it incidental pain: it was something he chose willingly, knowing full well how bad it would be. Instead, he went straight through it like a woman through the pain of labor, bringing to birth a new creation—a revelation of the promise of God in love.

My tooth is still sore, and I have to take antibiotics for a while, but at least I've started to have something done about it. (And we got the project finished up, regardless.)

Hopping Crosses

Was struggling all week with one hell of a case of anxiety, brought about in a good cause. If I may muddle up some metaphors, I was trying to go back and untangle an old and very nasty knot in my life, one that had done great harm to me and others and in which I'd been intricately entangled. Going back to that knot (muddled metaphors coming!) took me through a personal landscape littered with spent ammunition, shellholes, and abandoned rusting ordnance. A very scary place for me. It has not been easy, and it will not be easy for quite a while yet. I'm sure this is the right thing to do—but I can't help being tense and edgy, short with my kids, and subject to fits of heart-banging, to nervous starts, and to sudden mini-explosions like corn popping.

So, sitting at the computer, unable even to play a stupid game of gin rummy and getting all wired up about that as well, I resolved to give over my anxiety to God: here, God, *you* take it. I understand that, for some people, this decision immediately results in a great flood of peace and well-being. Some people are clearly better at this handing-over technique than I am—or maybe it's because I am such a slob at this religion business, can't even keep my Lent quarters-card up to date. . . . I handed my anxiety over, quite sincerely, several times, without the handover making any appreciable difference. I swear, sometimes you hand a thing over to God and God just looks at it thoughtfully, says, "Very interesting!" and hands it right back, saying, "Here you go. Enjoy."

Sigh.

I remember, then, a conversation I had about four-five years ago with a dear friend, a rotund half-Hungarian Presbyterian minister named George, who is still one of my saints-on-earth people. We'd been talking about another problem that I'd been trying to hand over to God, without success, and George said: "You try to hand this cross you're carrying over to God. You try to put it down. But it doesn't *want* to be put down. This cross wants you to keep on carrying it, even though you shouldn't. Just think of that cross you're trying to put down, and see it as hopping down the road after you. And keep hold of a rolled-up newspaper, in your mind. That cross is going to keep on hopping after you, jumping up, demanding to be carried. When it does that, you turn around and hit it with the newspaper, like hitting a badly behaved puppy across the snout to make it stop jumping up. And tell it that it belongs to God, and you aren't God."

My hopping cross of anxiety wanted to cling to me, to hang on tight; it didn't want to go to God, because God would put it to death and who likes dying? So much of our sinfulness—the stuff St. Paul means when he says, "I do things that I don't want to do, and I don't know why"—is like this. It's as though it (whatever it is—anxiety, grief, grievance, obsession) takes on a life of its own, a life that possesses our own lives in ways we don't like but seem helpless to do anything about. Our giving it to God will put it to death, and it clings the harder, not wanting to die.

Of course, the hardest thing is then to shift and see that my anxiety really is part of *me*, not an outside thing at all. A piece of my own soul is hopping after me, and that's what I have to find some way of giving over to God. There's some comfort in two things: first, that God knows I can't do it all today, and second, that God knows where it's coming from and why I'm having such trouble with it.

Could be that I'm not able to give this particular hopping cross up now because I have some learning to do; if so, I must do my best to carry the thing as patiently as I can and figure out what it is that I'm supposed to be doing in my soul-work. Could be that something needs to change—some circumstance I don't know about, some other portion of my soul—before I can be at peace again.

I have to trust that God knows exactly what God's doing, even if I don't, that God will look after me *and* my anxiety, and that God will relieve me of the latter in God's good time. In the mean-time, sometimes all a person can do is just to keep putting one foot ahead of the other for a while, and maybe that's what God wants me to do about this one, for now.

But I still lost the gin game.

Fool's Gold

(I'm going to have to fictionalize all of what follows somewhat, or people may come after me with baseball bats; so please don't take any of this literally. . . .)

My desk is not a tidy place. In fact, cascades of paper tumble regularly to the floor, and the joke is that I can't find my glasses because I put them on my desk and they sank without a trace. But sometimes a strange order erupts into things, and so it was the other day, when my desk had upon it:

+ a document I was editing, a major PR thingie for an agency we'll call XYZ;
+ the front pages of the day's newspaper; and
+ a letter written by person A to person B, which B had given me to read

Yes, they all connect. The PR document loudly and earnestly proclaims XYZ's undying devotion to (shall we say?) Environmentally Sound Management. The newspaper had a major story on how XYZ's senior management had grossly interfered with and even harassed XYZ's employees who were trying actually to *do* Environmentally Sound Management, while XYZ was really promoting get-rich-quick business interests.

The letter from A to B was an incredibly nasty letter, full of rage and thrown-about accusations and blame and guilt-making manipulation. Objectively speaking, it was quite vicious. But on the second to last page the writer A proclaimed that he is a good and loving person, a deeply sensitive person, who hurts because he cares so much about people and who just cares too deeply about B not to want to help B correct B's faults.

Huh?

Right. Sure. Uh-huh.

I don't think anyone ever starts out with the intention of being a hypocrite. Or maybe some people do; I've never encountered anyone like that, though. Strangely, I'm absolutely certain that A is convinced that he is indeed good and loving, sensitive and caring, and only concerned for B's welfare—although you sure couldn't tell that from the letter, which was a real stinker.

I suspect in XYZ's case it's a little more conscious; it's called "spin doctoring." If we make the right noises, put up the right decorations, maybe we can distract people's attention from our more than tiny failure to make good on what we're promising. You can perhaps fool enough of the people enough of the time ... I don't know how deep the self-deception goes among XYZ's managers— probably not as deep as A's self-deception, which is solid as the rock of Gibraltar. You never know, though. Could be they honestly believe in their dedication to Environmentally Sound Management—with a few regrettably necessary exceptions....

The fact is, though, that both A and the senior management of XYZ are proclaiming something which is not the truth, and they should, realistically, be able to see some problems with their own performance—their praxis. Their walk and their talk don't match up. Quite spectacularly not, in fact. (Of course Christians never have this problem, ohnononono...who, us?)

It all comes down to a Great Underlying Truth: fool's gold is cheaper than real gold.

It's also less ductile, of course; you can't do much with fool's gold except admire the glitter. Ultimately it doesn't do anything except sit there looking pretty—but it does *look* pretty. And sometimes that's what a person wants the most—to look pretty.

XYZ's reasons for wanting to look pretty are complex and sinuous and highly political. A's reasons for wanting to look pretty are, I suspect, rather more straightforward, and much, much sadder. But in both cases, faced with a choice between the easy way plus the right look and the tough way, they've opted for the first. It's far easier for XYZ to proclaim its high ideals than it is actually to try to live up to them. Real praxis could cost XYZ its support in the business world, which sees "environment" as a four-letter word. It's far easier for A to proclaim that he's a good and loving person that it is for him actually to behave in loving ways. Real praxis could involve looking at the real rage washing through the letter—and A cannot afford to accept ownership of that rage, at a guess.

Easier to make the right noises; easier to present the correct look. And maybe much of the time that's enough. Was the Russian Empress Catherine actually fooled by the dressed-up happy cardboard villages that her lover Potemkin put along her way, to show how prosperous the serfs were? Or did she know they were fake, and accept the deceit for what it was worth? I don't know. If she knowingly accepted the deceit, I suppose she was a bit worse than if she'd honestly been deceived—but she was also an extremely intelligent, very shrewd woman. So which is worse, then: refusing to use the head God gave you to see reality; or seeing reality and refusing to acknowledge it? I honestly don't have a clue.

Of course we all do this. Is there a person present who doesn't buff up his or her public image just a trifle? Are we all prepared to belch and scratch in public? To exhibit our imperfections, our neuroses, our secret longings? I don't think so, and I don't think this is a bad thing. Good manners may not be scrupulously honest, but they do grease the skids of existence.

Still, there's a line of sorts, one separating a light coat of much-needed varnish from a failure to accord with Big Obvious Important Truth, and both XYZ and person A are on the wrong side of that line. And they're there to protect themselves—XYZ from getting in trouble with business; A (I suspect—I can't know, of course) from his own personal dragons, which were almost audibly yipping in the background throughout that letter.

But ultimately the measures we take to protect our egos at the cost of reality won't work. The PR document, however skillfully I spin it, won't do XYZ any good. The press is simply too sharp-nosed; it will scent the deep underlying falsehood. It will rip through my carefully crafted phrases looking for the substance that has an interesting sharp smell, something the reader can smack his or her lips over.

A, on the other hand, may never have to face those yipping dragons. His deceit is deeper and more inward, and it's rooted in a profound and sad fragility. If he honestly felt loving, maybe he wouldn't have to yell about it quite so persistently. But his self-justifying outburst cost him B's love, and that was of some importance. That's his reality check.

If we know ourselves to be truly loved by God, we can actually afford to be honest; we needn't invest in window dressing to cover up our inner insufficiency. It's called integrity, and it means an inner oneness. Self and ego aren't separate, the one presented to the public, the other is hidden away at home where it's safe. There is only the person, no persona.

We don't *need* to trade in fool's gold; we've had enough of the real stuff poured into our lap, a shower of such true and honest love as could overwhelm us if we could ever face straight into it—which we can't; we can only glance at it sideways now and again. We can afford to give prodigally of that love, to be truly loving people, working at love more than proclaiming it, because we are only the instruments allowing Love to flow through.

I'm sorry for them, both XYZ and A—sorrier for the individual than for the agency, because his failure is more complete. Ultimately, both will have to come to terms with their insistence on offering fool's gold when they'd promised the true metal—but that's between them and God in the end. It's not my business.

But one thing I do know, and know well: when we deceive, we do harm. When we promise gold and deliver fool's gold, we debase the currency. Better, I think, to promise less and deliver on our promises—that way, at least, we can do no harm, except (perhaps) to our egos or our own self-will.

I put the edited document into an envelope to take back to the office, dropped the newspaper in the bag for recycling, set the letter aside to give back to its owner next time I see B. The confluence was temporary and breaks easily. The pattern, sadly, is not.

Customary Things

A neighbor hired my senior son Ross and his best friend Chris to carry a load of cordwood from his driveway to his basement and stack it. Ross schlepped; Chris, who had been taught the art by his grandfather, stacked.

Stacking cordwood has to be done right, the big pieces *here* and the small ones *there*, knots turned to the side, pieces placed with care, so the stack is tight and solid and stable. I helped at one point, tossing sticks of firewood down the neighbor's basement stairs—noisy work, but oddly satisfying.

Watching the boys stack wood made me think of things like darning socks or stooking hay—arts of living that my great-grandparents would have taken utterly for granted and my great-grandchildren (if I have any) may be as utterly unacquainted with. My father's mother, I believe, still knew how to make her own laundry soap. I can do some of the old things—making bread by hand, for example, or brewing black ale—but I cannot for the life of me hand-stitch a solid buttonhole, as any of my foremothers could.

Nor do I want to, particularly. Maybe we're losing some old skills, but do we really need them?

On the other hand:

On Thursday, off on a retreat, I sat and listened to an Algonquin elder whose European name is Linda. She brought to our circle some of her people's traditions, strong, old, and handsome. There was nothing artificial or wrong about her singing or teaching or smudging us with burnt sage; it was all right and natural, full of meaning, uniting us with a great and patient quietness.

The word "liturgy" means "the work of the people." Ross and Chris's work was to build a stack of firewood. Because that is an ancient occupation, and our forebears were not fools, doing it according to tradition made a great deal of sense. Linda's work was to bring together a circle of white people, helping us communicate in ways that were gentle, spiritual, honest, and nonthreatening. To do this, she brought to bear her own traditions—but she bent them for our sake, because we don't know them and not all of them would be appropriate for this work. She bent them intelligently, and she told us where she was bending them, but she accepted that the work itself mattered so much that the Creator would not mind the bending.

What matters in our liturgy is the nature of the work; how it's performed is important, but not (to my mind) sacred. It matters that we do the work well, because it is work for each other and God; but it's also important to remember that the end matters more than the means. The end is love, not beauty and propriety; the end is the pain of inclusion, not the luxury of exclusiveness.

I love singing the Sursum Corda at the beginning of the Prayer of Consecration in the Eucharist, the ancient duet between priest and congregation:

> *The Lord be with you.*
> And with your spirit.
> *Lift up your hearts.*
> We lift them up to the Lord.
> *Let us give thanks to the Lord our God.*
> It is right to give our thanks and praise.

Those words link me to others around the world and far back in time; that prayer is very ancient. In my church, we sing it in contemporary English, to a contemporary setting, plain but attractive. The meaning is the same, however, and it's the meaning that matters. I'm glad that other churches preserve the older style, but I don't think it's essential to the purpose of the prayer. God hears it said or sung or chanted, in English or Swahili or Latin or Inuktitut, in words old or new. The prayer is the same. How we say it is mutable, as we are.

Any change is a small death, and it's wrong either to fail to mourn or to wallow in mourning; it's a process that has to be got through—but then we move on. God alone is eternal, unchanging; we can't expect the church to be God that way. I think we're equally wrong to worship tradition as we are to worship novelty. Neither is God, after all. Change will come, inevitably, because we people of God are organic, and anything organic is static only if it's dead. We will change (I hope!) with the direction of the Holy Spirit, who should be calling the shots. But life calls us to the process of becoming, not to looking back and staying where we were.

Fewer people now know how to build a stack of cordwood, but the knowledge is still with us, very much alive. I'm glad Ross learned how—just as I'm glad he can do computer programming. There are not as many Algonquin elders as there once were, but people like Linda are taking the tradition from their elders and handing it on to others. I will know in future never to leave the circle when an Algonquin elder is present. I will know to sit when the elder sits and stand when he or she stands, to put a small helping of each food served at a meal out under a tree to the east of the meeting place, and to hug with left sides together, because the heart is on the left side. I'm glad to know these things. They too matter, not so much for what they are, as for what they represent: respect and love.

But what matters more is what breathes into and out of our souls while we do these customary things. That, after all, is what God cares for.

Dump Run

It is a matter of small pride in this household that we only put out one bag of garbage per week, and not a full bag, either. Instead, once every couple of weeks I load up the car with cardboard, paper, glass, tin cans, and plastic (having already composted what's compostable) and head out for the town dump.

I did that yesterday, driving out through a dun and rain-soaked landscape that should have been depressing and was, instead, rich with quiet colors, slashed with the black of the winter-plowed fields. I like the dump run. I like the sense that I'm doing the right thing and purging my household of some of its litter and clutter. I like the guy who runs the dump, a small wiry bearded man who does his work carefully and well; he seems alert and thoughtful and very kind. People doing their dump runs smile at each other as we offload our recyclables. It's one of those quietly sociable things, and the ugliness of it is a comfortable ugliness, like my comfortable ugly old parka.

I wished yesterday that I could hand the dump man all my

fears and anxieties and say, "Here, take these and do something with them. Put them in with the plastics for recycling. Run the backhoe over them and crush them to bits, and then bury them deep in the sand of the landfill. If all else fails, let them blow away over the landscape, for Nature herself to process slowly." I wish I could hand my worries over one lump at a time, saying, "Here, take this one, and this one here, and that one," so that they no longer cause me to freeze in my tracks, or to stumble, or to sprint panic-stricken in all the wrong directions, or to lash out when I'm at my most despairing. While I'm at it, I wouldn't mind handing the dump man what other people's fear has done to me, too, and what wrong my fear has done to others.

I'm not talking about the reasonable sort of fear we feel when we've done something wrong and know we're going to have to set-tle up, or the fear we naturally feel when people we love (ourselves included!) are in danger, or normal responsible-type concern of the sort that does insist on health insurance, basic dentistry, and pay-ing the bills. That's not fear; that's prudence.

But there's another sort of fear that paralyzes us, keeps us from moving and unfolding as we know we should, and that's not ex-ternal; it comes from deep inside us. Maybe we've learned the hard way to be afraid. Maybe it's something inside us that we're afraid of. Maybe we find it easier to displace our fear on somebody else and hate that somebody—classic scapegoating. Maybe we've played the scapegoat and have accepted the guilt that really isn't ours. Maybe we've learned the hard way not to be trusting.

Or maybe it's just the standard sense of being torn: wanting God's love, fearing God's insight; wanting human love, fearing intimacy; wanting success and being afraid of what it may cost us; wanting simplicity and fearing what we may have to give up to get it. We are complex creatures, full of contradictions and paradoxes, and the more aware we are, the more we're aware of how cross-grained we are. We've eaten of the Tree of the Knowledge of Good and Evil and the net result is that we're usually plunging off in all directions.

In strict moderation, maybe this equivocation isn't entirely a bad thing either. The healthy people I know—the ones I respect—seem to allow themselves to be less than fully certain without being paralyzed. They're honest about having their fears, but they also face into them without running away. They debate within themselves and with others the right course of conduct, neither jumping for the simple answer nor being frozen into inaction. They haven't got the easy answers, but they're willing to go ahead as best they can. They know they cannot say, "Do this, and it will all come out right." They are prepared to put a lot of effort and pain into making decisions, while paradoxically trusting that, in God's hand and God's time, it will all come round right.

Christ too went through a patch of real fear in the Garden before he walked straight into the arms of his passion and death. Maybe all he asks of us is something approaching his own honesty and effort. We're human, and it's when we turn our backs on humanity—our own or others'—that we start behaving in ways that do harm. It never hurts to confess that we're imperfect or fearful or mourning or uncertain or unsure of ourselves. It was the people who are questing and confused, not the group with all the answers, that Christ called blessed. The harm comes when we claim a perfection—including a courage!—that is not in fact ours. As Wagner pointed out, a person who's totally fearless isn't human.

I can only walk this journey, one step at a time, knowing that God keeps me company, however murky the days may seem sometimes. For this is the pattern of the Christ, and that's the pattern I have promised to follow, believing that this way will take me, through whatever murkiness, toward the Light. God came to earth to prove to us that we do, in fact, have nothing *really* to fear, and He went to extraordinary lengths to prove His point. With that hope clutched tight, I think—I hope—I can confront fear and walk right through it, and out the other side.

Hardscrabble

It's hard to imagine what it must have been like for the first settlers around here. We're in-between country, with the harshly
beautiful but obviously unfarmable Canadian Shield on our west,
and rich, flat, dull Laurentian bottomland on the east. It's not obvious that the soil hereabouts isn't really very good, except in
patches. Back a hundred and fifty years ago, the surveyors marked
it all off in neat concessions and lots and the government gave it
out in grants. Settlers got their parcels and went through the heart-
breaking, horrendous labor of clearing the land. And they tried to
farm it, and could get by on it, just barely—but the farms didn't
prosper, except for those few that happened to find pockets of
good soil. No fault of the farmers, but nobody saw it that way.

The assumption was that if you worked hard enough, had
enough courage, were strong, did your duty, didn't break under the
load, then you would succeed. And, to a degree, the assumption
was right—for the people clearing the rich Laurentian bottomlands.
But farming here mostly didn't work because of the soil, not the

effort or ethic. Most of the old farms have been abandoned and have gone back to scrub timber, because God never meant this land to be farmed. That didn't stop people from making the assumption, though, and they cited the handful of successful farms as evidence.

And they also accepted the logical extension of the assumption: if you failed at farming, it must be because you didn't work hard enough, were a weakling, didn't do your duty, broke under the load. I still remember reading an academic analysis of why Irish settlers failed in Montague Township, which really *is* in the Canadian Shield. The academic historian who wrote it footled lavishly about with all sorts of cultural factors peculiar to the Irish, but it doesn't seem to have occurred to him to go out and *look* at what they were working with. In Montague Township, what isn't rock is bog. And vice versa. You'd have trouble raising a good crop of alder in that country.

That hardscrabble ethic sank into the local culture, and in fact it's extremely common. We judge others without mercy because we subject them to our own assumptions without looking at what they have to work with. Nor do we ask if our assumptions are, in fact, reasonable ones. I remember once being sternly informed by a severe young woman that the ONLY way to clean a kitchen floor was on hands and knees with a particular type of detergent, weekly, first pulling out the stove and fridge and meticulously cleaning underneath them, and anyone who operated differently was clearly All Wrong and Slovenly. She was an extreme example of a very common human phenomenon. We simply assume that people who don't meet our standards (the Only Reasonable

Standards, of course!) must be weak and feckless, slackers, negligent in their duty. It doesn't occur to us to ask if our standards are, in fact, reasonable—any more than it occurred to people judging the failed farms to ask if the land was suitable for farming.

It doesn't seem to occur to us, either, that it would be perfectly reasonable for others to turn around and judge us by *their* standards, which are (naturally) the Only Reasonable Standards, by which we might have a few deficiencies ourselves. You could, for example, examine the hardscrabble culture and condemn it for being inbred, culturally narrow, and backward—but God forbid anyone should make those sorts of comparisons. That severe young woman disciplined her children in ways that could have got her in trouble with Children's Aid—but God forbid anyone should judge her maternal behavior.

We have the "right," we think, to prophesy righteously for others, to tell them exactly what their sins are, because we know THE TRUTH—but God forbid anyone should look at us too closely. We're allowed to turn the klieg lights on others while protecting our own treasured darkness from detailed examination. "I am honest; you are critical; they are emotionally abusive."

The poor aren't all good or all bad. People can be broken without being despicably weak—in fact, in some ways, the broken may be stronger and healthier than those who resist breaking with all their might. The race is not always to the swift, nor the contest to the strong. Gentleness is not always weakness, but sometimes a deeper form of strength. There's more, much more, to life than Duty, and our greater duty is more to the soul's formation than to the correctly clean kitchen floor—or, for that matter, the meticulously celebrated church service or perfect piece of dogma.

Of course the hardscrabble ethic stems from anger—a deep underlying harsh rage, unexamined and undigested and merely passed from one generation to another: "I have suffered, and I want others to suffer too so that I'm not alone in my suffering; I feel inadequate, so I will judge others as less than myself so that I'll feel better about my inadequacy." Such a sorry way to be. . . .

The ethic also sees suffering as redemptive in and of itself: "I am good and noble *because* I suffer, and those who don't suffer are failures compared to me." But in fact suffering doesn't redeem us; we redeem it, by turning it toward the Light and Love. If we worship suffering for itself, set it up as a god, then we're far more apt to fall into the Sin of Anger (and impose our cruelty on other people) than to find redemption. We're apt to set up hierarchies of suffering—a sort of Great Chain of Suffering, in which we're all glancing covertly around, trying to figure out where we are in the Suffering scheme of things, instead of simply facing whatever it is we have to face, and getting on with what has to be got on with, if that makes sense. We're also apt to impose quite unnecessary Suffering upon others for their own good, without much asking whether in fact it *is* for their own good, or for our own covert needs. Not good stuff.

Suffering is more or less inevitable in life, but it's not redemptive unless we allow God to make good use of it. We can, instead, revel in suffering, wallow in it out of vanity and self-righteousness, and that sort of suffering is anything but redemptive. As usual, it's like sex or nuclear power: it's not the thing in itself that's good or bad, but how we use it and what we let it make of us.

Suffering, properly used, may make us stronger, but it will also make us gentler—and while the hardscrabble ethic may judge gentleness as weakness or spiritual flabbiness, in fact that true gentleness, which is as wholesome and sweet as a good apple, is (to my mind) the mark of far deeper strength and of true maturity of faith. After all, Christ blessed the meek, not the rigidly righteous in their resentment and self-importance. Blessed is that gentleness, for it redeems suffering and makes it God's own property.

The sorry thing about the hardscrabble farms isn't that they failed—they were foredoomed to do that—but that they left a sort of dour, judgmental, harsh, unforgiving taste to the local culture that took a long, long time to wear off. A gentler culture has grown up hereabouts, thank God, one that is moving toward seeing people in the fullness of their humanity, instead of in high-contrast simple black and white. The community has turned away toward a warmer, less judgmental ethic than the hardscrabble one. That's why I like the place.

But watch for the hardscrabble ethic, for it still flourishes. At least the earth hereabouts has begun to recover. It may take the human spirit longer.

What Matters

Standing in the sunlit kitchen a moment ago, frosting a lemon cake—and suddenly I was back thirty years, three states, two provinces, and a country change ago, in the big rectory kitchen, frosting a cake. It seemed so desperately important then to do it neatly. I remember the frustration; I could do the gluing-together frosting between the layers, but the top of the top layer tended to disintegrate under my hasty spatula and the sides were always a mess. I was in despair; it seemed so very important.

I could smile over the memory. I still frost a cake messily; I've merely learned that it doesn't matter. There are those for whom it does matter, and who will do this small job better than I will. There are other small jobs, like ironing a man's shirt, that I do better than many other people. But in the great scheme of things, a neatly frosted cake really isn't terribly important. There is only so much energy a person has to invest in things, and cake-frosting is low on my personal totem pole.

In the great scheme of things, in some twenty or thirty years or so, I will have to answer to God for what I've made of what He has given me. God makes it clear that He does expect us to do the best with what we're given—that's proper stewardship. I will have to answer for it if, for example, I let my beautiful old house fall down around my ears because I can't be bothered to take care of it, or if I injure the world God made by being environmentally irresponsible.

But am I going to have to answer to God for lemon-cake frosting? Obviously that's silly. I am, of course, going to have to answer to God for how I've behaved as a child, a mother, a worker, a lover, a friend. If I muff a piece of work, that should concern me because of the effect my failure has on others. If I fail in love toward someone who's one of mine to love, obviously that should concern me even more.

It's hard sorting out what should matter from what shouldn't. Perhaps one of the many, many reasons Christ spoke so highly of the poor and dispossessed is that, for them, the choices tend to be basic and straightforward. When you're at a level where food and shelter are in question, then the precise color of the drapes isn't apt to be much of a worry to you. That's one end of the spectrum; at the other is (perhaps) the sort of person whose mind can be deeply occupied—even driven into deep and genuine distress—by worrying whether the ribbons on the gift-wrapped package are, in fact, the exactly correct shade of rose or should have been pale lilac. Poverty does, after all, sometimes help to strip things down to their beautiful bare bones. If God may feel especially near to those wandering in the desert, perhaps it's because the air is so clear and there aren't so many distractions.

But most of us fall somewhere in the middle, and the things that get our knickers in a twist are, in fact, precisely the choices we know we're going to have to answer for later on. Should I take a stand that may cost me part of my social life? Should I invest for my old age or give more to charity? Should I express anger when someone crosses my boundaries or forgive and keep my silence? Should I stay in this church, where I'm miserable but needed? Should I leave this job, this town, this marriage? These things do matter, because it's in decisions like these that we form our own souls and profoundly affect the people whose lives touch ours.

What should matter to us is making these choices in obedience to God's will for us—and the problem, of course, is that we have to figure out whether that means left or right at the next corner. God does not do skywriting, more's the pity. What we have to hang on to and work with is, first and foremost, the Great Commandment. It's the execution that's often so damned tricky.

What we may fail to see, however, is that the rightness or wrongness of our final choices may in fact matter less than the process we're willing to put ourselves through to get there: "the journey, not the arrival, matters." For it's in struggling with these decisions, trying to act responsibly and lovingly, that we do the work of making ourselves a more fit offering to Him who gave us the raw materials we work with.

So: I can start by not worrying about cake frosting, which is an easy thing to let go of, and then try not to worry about other things that I know shouldn't stand between me and God or between me and my fellow human beings. I can concentrate on what's on my plate for today, making the most of what the day gives me to work with, and keeping the Great Commandment in the back of my mind. I will have to answer for what I do, the choices I make—but I will be answering to One who loves me. Of that, I am quite sure.

Part Three

High Winter

Hands On

Yesterday was our star designer's last day at work; she's off to have her first baby sometime early in the new year. I'm looking forward to meeting the kid when she has it, and to holding a baby again. It surprised me, when my own two were born, how satisfying I found baby-holding. I loved the sheer feel of them, the weight and warmth, the particular baby smell, the fine skin, that most satisfying heaviness and hard roundness of a small head fitted into the hollow of my shoulder. I've always been hands-on with my kids (the First Law of Parenthood: when in doubt, cuddle). My younger one is almost too big and almost too old to be a lap-cat, but he's still a spectacular hugger and physically very affectionate.

Funny how love seeks to be physical. It's not true of everyone, but it is very common for people to want to touch or hug or pat or cuddle the people they love, and to need to be touched or hugged or patted or cuddled, just to feel the warmth and weight of being loved. Of course hugs can be as false as any other human

81

behavior—think of Judas kissing Jesus—but when the love is real, it often seems to get across best with the human skin on it. As John Donne wrote:

So must pure lovers' souls descend
T'affections and to faculties
Which sense may reach and apprehend
Else a great Prince in prison lies.

Being the sort of young man he was as a young man, Donne was *certainly* talking about sex. But love's need to get hands-on goes further and broader and deeper than that. Babies deprived of touch fail to thrive and may even die. Ill people given touch therapy recover faster. I've run into people who were touch-starved—who soaked up loving touch as bone-dry earth soaks up rain. Light, loving touch calms anxiety; it strokes away tensions. It speaks to body and mind, both at the same time, whispering reassurance and deep care.

It may have been with this in mind that God chose to em-body God—and as an infant, the one form of human that MUST be touched. You might be hands-off with the sort of Messiah the Jews had been expecting, the warrior and king. But not with babies. They must be handled, carried, nursed, changed, fed, dressed, bathed, and (if you're doing this right) played with and cuddled. And they evoke this sort of love from the people who care for them.

God brought God's love to earth and gave it to us, hands-on, by the most surprising route: by being helplessly lovable, as only infants can be.

It's not surprising that the two universal Christian sacraments are the ones involving commonplace physical things—bathing and eating. In Baptism and Holy Communion, God touches our bodies in love, using these gifts of nature to wash and feed us as a parent washes and feeds a child. The water runs cold on the skin, wetting a baby's soft hair; the sacramental oil soaks into the skin's pores. We chew and sip and swallow bread and wine, and the molecules of the elements become elements of our bodies: grace mixed in with complex carbohydrates; esters and alcohol and acids and love, inseparable. Who knows? Most of an atom is space, after all, and who knows what enters those spaces when we invoke God's blessing on the physical stuff of sacraments?

God got hands-on with us, starting with the birth we're about to celebrate at Christmas, and we remember and pass on that loving touch through the touch of sacramental rites. God feeds and waters us, body and soul. God is in loving touch when we tend each other—in a mother nursing her child, in the grasp of a friend's hand, in holding someone who's crying, in stroking a loved one's hair, in a child's jumping up to be hugged, in compassionate touch-gift to the sick, in cradling the dying.

Love came down at Christmas and put a warm, breathing, needy, loving, and very human skin on; and that love still holds us firmly, kindly, hands-on: body and soul.

Lights

Went last night to deliver a Christmas present to a friend out in the country. This last week, we've had remarkable weather, mild and open, sunny by day with an almost springlike cyan-blue sky, sunsets streaked apricot and rose, and a ripe full moon. Each night I've looked out on a landscape strangely blue with moon on snow. But yesterday was cloudy, and last night the sky was thoroughly occluded. As I drove west to my friend's house, the only light was the dirty-ocher town glow of the city to the north. For the rest, without my car lights, I doubt I could have seen my hand before my face. In the country, when it gets dark, it gets DARK.

Except for the Christmas lights . . . Along my street heading out of town, along the county highway, there they were—not every house lit up, but many houses. People's Christmas lights vary, quite wildly, from the neatly prosaic to the whopping-baroque. I suspect they say something about the people who put them up. What *do* you make of someone who puts up precisely ten red bulbs, ten blue, ten red, ten blue, in a scrupulously neat row along the eaves-troughs? Ah—there's a romantic with good taste: an old brick farm-house with pure white lights draped gracefully among its shrubs and wound through the gingerbread trim on the porch. Some peo-ple go a little crazy and sling dozens of lights all over the place. Others are restrained. Some are monochrome red or blue; most are variegated. But all in all, it makes for a pretty display. The variety is part of the pleasure.

One of the better side effects of having lived through Interesting Times is that, properly received and digested, a few solid whomps upside a person's skull may help to clear the mind of a great many foolish notions. I feel blessedly relieved of any need to assess an-other person's Christianity at Christmastide. It is none of my busi-ness whether the people in these houses are in a state of grace or not. It need not disturb my inner *wa* if they're enjoying "I Saw Mommy Kissing Santa Claus" instead of "Once in Royal David's City." If they worship Santa Claus or the "Spirit of Christmas" in-stead of the Christ Child, I can at least see that there's at least a trace of the Christ Child in what they worship—in the message of love and generosity, in the willingness to stop in front of Mystery, in the longing for that Something that Christians find in the manger. Whether or not they know it, Christ was born and died for my neighbors. The essential thing is that I know that he did it for me.

But the lights . . . the lights *do* something. They have a curious effect on the dark around them. It's as though something from them flows out into it. The dark among these strands of bright-ness is somehow different from the plainer, flatter dark over fields and woods and cedar swamps. This dark is softer; it's less sheerly impenetrable and more full of playfulness, even mischief. Dark can be the midnight blue against which stars are shot silver. Or it can be just plain dark.

Whatever specific motive is behind them, whatever people think as they put them up, the lights are an offering to God, an oblation of cheerful beauty at the darkest time of the Canadian winter. Whatever Christmas has turned into, it has at least made that oblation something that my neighbors do every year, without question but with deep enjoyment.

Not everyone will be making this gift. Some are sick in body or mind, or mourning, or alone. They are in the dark for a greater or lesser time, not by choice; for now, they feel they have nothing to make the oblation with. Others don't feel the need for the lights, some because they are so deep into the Light that lights are un-necessary, others for different reasons. Some say, "What's the prac-tical good of them?" They deny the need to make an offering at all. And then there are those who are full of resentment or bitter-ness or self-centeredness. They have chosen the dark and the dark abides with them, because God leaves us free to choose the Light or the dark.

We can be lights, by our witness of the Love of God to this world, which sometimes seems nothing but night. We can be steady in that light-giving; and then, even if the darkness doesn't go away, it's softened and made somewhat less impenetrable and more hopeful near us, at least for a time. And we will have shown other people how it's done, this light-giving. That's worth some-thing, I think.

The lights have lent grace to this plain place, and something of that grace will linger even after people take the strands down and the year turns around and the days get longer again. But for those of us who believe, who are willing to take the risk of faith, the light steadies and strengthens and grows, from a small flame in the dark, until it explodes in glory at the next great feast: the Resurrection.

All Poor Men
and Humble

(CHRISTMAS 1996)

She moves quietly around the poky apartment, a small blond woman in her early thirties, chunky, tired-looking, neither pretty nor plain—the sort of person you look right past on the bus without ever noticing. She glances into her kids' room, listening to their even breathing as they sleep, finishes the dishes, starts a cigarette and puts it out after a couple of puffs, saving the rest for later—she's planning to give up smoking for New Year's and has been cutting down. She thinks about calling her parents, but she really can't afford long distance; they'll call her tomorrow.

This year there's not much under the tree, and nothing for her that she didn't buy herself and wrap, doing it all on the cheap. Her parish donated some things for the kids, but they didn't ask what her children liked or needed, so she thanked the outreach committee person and quietly gave the too small clothes and the too young toys to another needy family. Still, it was better than it had been. Last year, for the last time ever, she'd weathered the brunt of her husband's annual "I hate Christmas" explosion, getting the kids stowed out of range and cleaning up the wreckage afterward, and had then patiently steered him through the bout of self-pitying depression that always followed his rages. At least—thank God!—she can finally put an end to that particular Christmas tradition. They're better off this way, hard as it is sometimes.

She rarely watches TV. Instead, she switches on the radio, keeping the volume low, taking up a magazine. But the carols she's hearing only make her eyes leak; loneliness makes her feel as though her whole core is empty and aching. Abruptly, she doubles over with a sudden burst of anguish rising slowly up from some depth—she doesn't know where or what it comes from. It's like old-fashioned milk pudding coming up to a slow boil. She has learned to breathe her way through these fits of inexplicable pain, doing her crying silently for the kids' sake, not to upset them. She gets her breath back and turns the radio off, making her mind go blank. Getting up, she tidies the apartment, sorts papers, pausing sometimes to blow her nose. Staying busy helps.

What's hard—what she really has trouble handling without anger—are all the good, kind, well-intentioned people who wish her a joyous Christmas. Joy. Fat chance. With luck, she might get herself together enough to manage a shaky peace. With time it will get better—she's prepared to hope as much—but it's going to take a long time to get back to a state of mind where joy is possible at all. She tries to be charitable and good-natured, to accept the good wishes in the spirit in which they're intended. She doesn't want to be a grinch. But still, to be told "Cheer up! it's Christmas!" or "Get in the Christmas spirit!" feels like being slapped in the face with a wet flounder. Oh, pullleeeze!!

She had taken the kids to the parish pageant, which was a zoo, but she'll be missing Midnight Mass this year and probably for several years more. Forget finding a baby-sitter to come late on Christmas Eve; she'd never ask that of anyone. She'd thought about rousing the kids and taking them with her, but it means a long walk—buses aren't running this late—or a taxi ride she can't afford. She could have asked someone to take the three of them, but asking for help is so humiliating. . . . And it's rough on four- and six-year-olds to have their sleep interrupted. All three of them would pay for that the next day.

Part of her grieves, because she used to love Midnight Mass, but another part is shamefacedly relieved that she can't be there. These days, she feels as badly alienated from the great solemn ceremony of High Mass as from the commercialism in the shops. Oh, yes, a part of her loves and longs for the richness and splendor of the service, its weight and deep rich beauty, its sheer sensuality, all that it evokes. But another part of her wants to howl during the music, performed with such meticulous artistry. It's so beautiful, and she's so messed up and ordinary and untalented; how can she belong here? She's got nothing to give that could ever be wanted. What has it got to do with her? There seems to be as little room for her pain in her church as in the shopping malls, and that feeling of being disconnected from her community is so much harder to bear than mere poverty. Ach, that hurts. . . .

Feeling herself starting to slide into self-pity, which she despises, she remembers the people she knows who are worse off than herself; she thinks of those who are ill or dying, of the homeless, of the people who go into total helpless tailspins this time of year. She thinks of her neighbor, whose wife died several years ago on December 26 and who always goes through Christmas with a pinched, gray look. She even thinks, with a sort of detached pity, of her ex-husband. Yes, his behavior at Christmas was intolerable; but she knew he was only carrying on *his* family tradition. And now he's alone; at least she has the children.

She should get to bed, but she can't; she's too keyed up. Moving restlessly around the living room, she picks up the wreath her son had brought home from school. It's made of twisted dried grape vines—the sort that arts-and-crafts people use as a basis for elaborate decorations that will only hint at what's at the base. But her child had merely glued on some plain pine cones and twisted a couple of strands of thin crimson ribbon around the thing. He hadn't even glued on sparkles.

It's plain and awkward, almost barren-looking, except for the odd grace of the ribbons curling around the bare twigs. She'd thought about getting some nice ribbon and gold spray paint and sparkles, and sitting down with the boy to dress the wreath up a little, make it prettier, but then she'd decided that she liked it just the way it is. There is something about its spare plainness that she finds comforting. It has its ordinary grace. In its bareness and angularity, it minds her of the crown of thorns.

"Where is my joy this year?" she thinks, tenderly turning the wreath in her hands, tucking in an errant strand of ribbon. She thinks of the beautiful polychrome Madonna in her church, a treasure, a thing of rich and grave beauty—the graceful, slender, stylized woman in her azure cloak and golden crown, holding out a plump Christ-toddler on the palm of her hand, at a totally unnatural angle. Superwoman, she'd always thought with inner amusement. The Madonna's grave grace and beauty and rich color used to move her, and may move her again, but right now the image has nothing at all to say to her. It's all abstraction. She is too far from grace and beauty; for her, the plain twig wreath.

But if she's can't imagine the Madonna, she *can* think of a girl, hugely pregnant, wretchedly uncomfortable, far from home and mother and family, maybe panicking as she felt her pains start with nowhere safe and private to lie down to birth her first baby. She remembers how, during her own first labor, the intensity of the pangs had startled her, and she'd clung to her husband's hand, trying not to cry out, as much in fear as pain: how much more of this can I endure? But stopping was out of the question. Sort of like where she is right now. . . . She can think of the girl facing uncertainty: what have I got myself into? Will this turn out all right in the end? What have I done by saying *yes*?

She can think of the baby. She can think, with wonder, of God choosing to fit God's sizable self into this tiny, puny, dark red package with the unfocused solemn dark eyes, the wisps of black hair, and the wrinkled skin—God's weak little legs bowed by the womb's tough rubbery walls, God's head, mushed out of shape by the abrupt, no-nonsense squeeze of birth, wobbling helplessly on a thin stalk of a neck, God's voice a protesting squawky wail as the cold air rushed into the new wet lungs. . . . Maybe the baby had been hairy all over like her own firstborn, before the hair fell out and he stopped looking like a chimpanzee.

They had been poor too, and not really respectable, the parents—the baby conceived well before his mother's marriage, the parents forced to be refugees for years afterward. God had not only come down to dwell among humankind, as one of us; God had chosen to dwell among that portion of humankind that humankind doesn't have much, if any, use for. Not many people respect the poor, not even the poor. She herself felt like a loser a lot of the time. Yet God had chosen to keep company with people who would never be successful, who had nothing to distinguish them, who would never be much of anything, who would probably always have to live from one day to the next, barely getting by. He'd chosen us, when He could have been anyone he wanted to, she thinks.

The thought comforts her. She knows she should make up the sofa bed in the living room, where she sleeps, but suddenly she is so tired her bones feel like water and she aches all over. She yawns convulsively, shuddering. She turns off the apartment's lights, except those on the small tree in the corner of the room, and curls up, still in her thread-pulled unbecoming pink sweatsuit, on the unmade-up sofa. She pulls the shabby eiderdown over herself, tucking her feet up, shuddering with cold and bone-deep exhaustion, hugging herself for comfort and leaning her cheek against the rough, worn sofa fabric. Then, letting the quiet move from her core outward, she lies watching the tree's tiny blinking lights as she grows warm and sleepy.

On the verge of dozing off, she finds herself humming an old much-loved hymn in her small cracked alto—not one of the carols she'd been blasted by at every turn for the last month, not the splendid stuff being harmoniously intoned by the choir tonight, but a song as plain and spare and serviceable as her child's wreath:

A Place Like Any Other

All poor men and humble,
All lame men who stumble,
Come haste ye and be not afraid,
For Jesus our treasure
Whose love passes measure
In lowly poor manger was laid....

She sleeps.

Gray Sister

I found myself glancing down to check whether the person standing next to me in the hardware store lineup was carrying a purse. There was a purse. This confirmed my initial vague impression that this person was female. Otherwise, I couldn't have known for sure.

You see a few around town like this: women so worn down by poverty and who knows what that they begin to look androgynous. This one was short and spherical. She wore a greasy sheepskin cap with the earflaps dangling, a man's worn green fabric parka over gray jogging clothes, work gloves, shitkicker work boots—but probably not (given vaguely defined bulges slightly north of what had been her waist) a bra. Hair: short, straight, thin, greasy gray-brown streaks, probably cut at the kitchen sink. Face: grayish, lined, expressionless, lifeless; eyes brown, surrounded by liverish brown circles and sunk deep. Age: somewhere between forty and the grave.

I smiled tentatively, an unspoken apology for the sin of having

noticed her at all, and got in return the merest lifting of the corners of her caved-in mouth and slightly shy look. I don't know
why, but when she smiled, something about her—the color of her
eyes, I think—reminded me of the teenage girl in the doctor's office yesterday, as we both waited for our appointments. The girl
was a nice-looking child, not a beauty, but happy and attractive,
halfway between shy and friendly.

In my mind's eye, I could morph that child into this woman—
they were about the same height, with similar planes to their faces.
I could pad the child's graceful young waist around with the fat
that comes from trying to find comfort in sweet stuff, when there's
no other comfort to be had. The girl's round high breasts could fill
out and sag to her waist, flattened by the weight of sheer discour-
agement. The shy friendliness could dim and sink under too much
trouble over too long a time. After a while a person gives up; the
self-care goes all to hell, because why should a person care how
she looks, or even whether she's clean, when there's no love or
comfort? That's when you start seeing greasy lank hair and skin
gray from a bad diet and not enough soap.

But this gray sister of mine—she has a soul. And I haven't the
slightest idea what that soul is like. Except that there seemed a
touch of sweetness about the lines of her face, a kindness in her
shy eyes, patience in the weary set of her thick body as she waited.
A certain restfulness? I had a sudden notion of how her soul might
be: all worn and flattened and hopeless—but softened, not embit-
tered, by suffering. I don't know. I can only guess, and try to guess
kindly.

Maybe in knowledge of God's love for her—His gray child, all exhausted by life as she was—she might take in the sweet clear water of God's grace and gentle mercy. And then, just as her once young firm body had long since changed into this tired, unsexed shapelessness, so her soul might morph back to something as fresh with health and happiness as that young girl in the doctor's office, ready to laugh and be hopeful and dream and dance—no more a sad sack, but a strong young bride.

If she can turn her face toward God, then in the Life to Come, only God knows the grace and joy and beauty she could attain, as age follows age—growing with delightful slowness until her soul is the size of an archangel and so bright with glory that suns hide their darkness before her, confused by her light. For God has that power, if we will only listen.

The line moved forward, slowly. I paid for my piece of cook-ware; she paid for her lug wrench. We exchanged small smiles again, and went out into the bitter weather.

So What Else
Is New?

Winter's been slow off the blocks this year. Only now, in the New Year, do we have the Classic Canadian Landscape—long fields of snow, blue-shadowed and faintly mysterious against a sky of opalescent white. The woods are graceful, ghostly. Roads, stained gray with salt, vanish suddenly in snow squalls. There's that rhythm of reaching for the windshield wipers every time a heavy truck is oncoming in the other lane, to deal with the inevitable faceful of thrown-up slush; that continual watchout for patches of black ice. . . . It's winter. It's like that.

This is Canada, and anyone who chooses to live here is going to deal with winter because, inconvenient or not, it's a part of life the way it is. God is not going to alter the climate here for our convenience. If a person gets drunk and lies down in a back alley in Winnipeg in January, that person is apt to freeze to death by morning. Is this a tragedy? I suppose so. I just know it's inevitable.

Winter may be inconvenient, but it's innocent—as is gravity, as is biology. There is no evil in winter, no malice of intent; it's just a fact here. I've developed a certain love for its clean, matter-of-fact, hard-fisted realness. I certainly respect it. I don't think I could go winterless without feeling that I'd missed out on something substantial and important. But there's no sense shaking a fist at the sky when a foot of snow has made life more complicated. This is Canada. This is January. You expected maybe feathers?

So why do we try to make God accountable for tragedy? Where was it written that life would be easy? That life would be protective and simple and pain-free? Where was it promised us, if we live in this country, that the norm is summer (*sans* blackflies, naturally!) and that winter is an aberration? We go out without our gloves, and our fingers are cold and hurting; should we cry out that we're in pain? I could drive my car into the as yet unfrozen St. Lawrence, praying madly for God to save me, and when (not if!) the car sinks, has God betrayed me or failed to love me? I don't think so.

Of course there are injustices, and they are terribly painful; of course there is real evil, and it's human—people turning their backs on the Light and running in the direction of disintegration, doing huge harm on the way. Of course there are hearts banged and bruised and even broken, and trust deep-betrayed, and neglect and abuse, most of it out of painfully ordinary human failings—mostly sloth and the refusal to face reality with love and humility. The world is so full of humans doing things that we cannot possibly justify to God. Whatever makes us think that God needs to justify God's ways to man?

Does God look out for us? Yes, but not by protecting us—not by making miracles that require the rest of Creation to part company with reality. We don't encourage our children to grow by padding them round with feather pillows and cosseting their every whim and protecting them from every playground taunt; we expect them to learn to accept reality with toughness, patience, humor, and optimism and to become disciplined and responsible and loving and faithful people. Is that easy? No; it's a constant series of battles against normal human nature, which is anything but disciplined, responsible, loving, and faithful. Nobody said it would be easy.

Does God expect us to stay babies? No; and however much we want padding, God tends to take the feather pillows away; and sometimes, when we're being particularly pigheaded, God has to get pushy about it. Does tragedy occur? Yes; and it is terribly painful, and that pain is real, just as the bitter cold is real, and must be respected. But neither tragedy nor winter is evil, however harsh we feel them. Winter is winter. What matters is what we make of it.

What I *do* know is that God aches when we ache. God could choose not to suffer with us, but God chooses to take our suffering in and experience it alongside us. And God wills our pain away as I warm the chill out of a child's fingers with my hands. God wills the healing into us, if we will but put down our sense of wrong and anguish and be open to healing.

The love is there, light and kindness and warmth ready for us to turn into, as we come in out of the cold—if only we're willing to turn away from our own bitter inner winter.

Unvarnished

In a few short, carefully chosen phrases, I gave him my honest opinion of his character and behavior. I said exactly what I thought—the unvarnished truth, as I saw it. Straight from the hip. So.

Will you all, please, check your automatic assumption that what I said was negative?

Why is it that we always seem to brace ourselves, without even thinking about it, when someone says, "I'm going to be honest with you"? Experience, of course. Those words usually mean that Something Awful is about to get said—bad news, perhaps, but more likely a terrific chunk of criticism, deserved or un-.

This is really interesting. Stop and unpack this idea for a moment. We see honesty and love as being separate, opposite—

(But wait a moment. Let's not call it "love"; that's unfair to the word. We're not talking about love when we've separated it from honesty, but about Unconditional Positive Regard, the sort of feeling that strokes our soft and puffy egos. It is what the Germans would call *gemütlichkeit*: it is warm-fuzzy, and accuracy is not what interests it. It is to genuine love as cotton candy is to good nourishing bread. But we love it. We desperately desire it. It feels sooooo good, so good that we don't notice how demeaning it really is.

(Similarly, I don't think we can talk about "honesty" if we've separated all the love out into a separate strand. True honesty would force us to admit that others have genuinely good characteristics, real accomplishments, virtues and strengths, and the whole point of "I'm going to be honest with you" is to cut the other person down to size. It's not even legitimate criticism, because legitimate criticism includes elements of praise and recognition, just as real love has elements of rueful acceptance. So let's call it by its right name, which is the Crushing Put-down. We hate it. We desperately flee or reject or evade it. It feels sooooo bad, and we're so crushed by it that we don't notice how inaccurate and unfair it really is.)

At what point did we take that two-ply thing, honest love, and separate out into "love" on one hand and "honesty" on the other? Do that, and of course what you get is far, far less than the sum of its parts. When you tease a two-ply yarn apart, you're left with trash, because the strength and perfection of the yarn lie in the ply, not in the individual strands. You're left with a mere indeterminate wiggling line of throwaway fuzz.

We don't just do this with human love, trying to feed each other the sugary mess of Unconditional Positive Regard or the bitter brew of the Crushing Put-down (or, most interestingly, both to-gether, but as sugarcoated bitterness). Neither is nourishing or healthful. But worse still, we believe that God has to do it *our* way, which is limiting God in ways that I doubt God appreciates very much. We talk about "justice" and "mercy" as though they were separate items. The Bad Guys (them) are going to get Justice, which means eternal flames; the Good Guys (us) are going to get Mercy, which means pie in the sky. Or maybe it will be the other way around, and we're in for the painful part. . . .

Excuse me: I don't think so.

When we come before our Maker to account for what we have made of our souls, we will look into the face of Honest Love, a Love that sees us exactly as we are—in the rude nude, because there's no point pretending that God doesn't see straight through our fibs and self-deceptions and excuses and rationalizations. We are going to be Seen, and we are going to be Loved. Which is, when you think about it, really quite a terrifying prospect.

Imagine being loved for your love handles. Imagine being loved for your zits and stray hairs and the bags under your eyes and your fallen arches and sagging breasts and buttocks. Imagine being in the clothes-store dressing room, stripped to the skin, turned to face the mirror, and being told that you are unimaginably beautiful. Imagine God seeing and loving you completely, thoroughly, through and through, while knowing that you really did seriously screw up and hurt someone, quite badly and in utterly inexcusable ways. Oooh, that's scary. . . .

Imagine God seeing all the things you're secretly ashamed of and would rather not know about yourself, much less show to anyone else—your temper, your neediness, your laziness, your self-righteousness, your obsessive agenda, your selfishness, your emotional stinginess, your manipulative streak. Or imagine being loved for your deep longing for gentleness and love, your vulnerability and fearfulness, and your push-pull need/fear of true intimacy—all stuff that shames you deeply. Having God see all that could be hell on the ego.

No wonder we want to disassemble honest love into Unconditional Positive Regard and the Crushing Put-down. We do so hoping, praying, that God will somehow lose the second part and let our egos off the hook. We cannot imagine being seen truthfully and accepted truthfully. Love hurts our eyes with its gentle, penetrating light. We don't want to meet that quietly truthful gaze, as clear, candid, and unsparing as a child's.

We'd love to have all the warm fuzzies, but we don't want God (or anyone else, for that matter) to see us too clearly. God's deeply loving mercy can be hard to take, because the fact of the mercy part faces us with the plain inescapable fact that we need mercy so very, very badly. Or we pray to face only God's justice, bracing ourselves for what we expect—harsh, unsparing righteousness, which we can meet with our toughness and strength; because we do not want to admit that we're vulnerable children, in need of gentleness and tender care and healing. To be loved truly would leave us utterly undone, helpless and at sea.

Doesn't matter. We only want half the loaf; but God insists on giving us the whole: honest love. So what, for heaven's sake, are we going to do with it?

High Winter

———

Oh—just to finish the story:

The person I was being straight with was my elder kid, on the way into the city on his fourteenth birthday. In brief, carefully un-embarrassing terms (because you shouldn't gush at adolescent boys) I told him exactly what I think of him. Which is quite a lot.

Love and Water

The nice thing about the pool is that I don't feel like an idiot in it. It doesn't matter that I'm middle-aged and no beauty in a bathing suit; we're mostly much of a muchness physically, middle-aged women, more lumpy than curvaceous and mostly waist-free. It doesn't matter that I swim poorly and sink by the feet unless I work hard at treading water; we have Styrofoam floats to work with, so I can concentrate on the movements without worrying about drowning. It doesn't matter that my coordination is utterly hopeless; you can't fall over and hurt yourself in the water. And all movement in the water is graceful because water is Like That. It's all dance, no clumsiness. So the aquabics class is perfect.

I go twice weekly and play like a kid in the water, utterly without thought or care. The water takes over, the cool mass of it, the smell of chlorine, the resistance and soft solidity of it. We move with it and against it to the beat of the music, trading jokes, doing movements which are childlike in their silliness and get you nowhere—and yet are profoundly healthful. Swinging Styrofoam barbells through the water, treading it, pretending to jog or ski through it—utterly free, completely safe. We grunt and splash and laugh and are silent when the work is really hard, and sometimes, when the music's right, we sing as we scull in the warm water, looking out at the snow outside the pool-room windows.

I've always hated exercise because I'm terrible at it. I'm a physical idiot—no confidence to speak of, no coordination or motor memory. (The class joke is that I have to learn movements one limb at a time and everyone laughs when I finally GET IT!!!) I never learned to swim properly, and to me the water has been something both inviting and dangerous—a place of freedom where I don't know what to do with myself. A place I could love to be in, but where I felt preordained to be a failure.

Our play is, in fact, deeply serious and thoughtful, concentrating on muscle groups and carefully balanced—but it *feels* like silliness. I've watched good swimmers with awe: the big bunchy back and shoulder muscles propelling them through water with a neat and purposeful elegance. The very idea defeats me. But we don't do that. We're foolish by comparison, and that, to me, is such a rest.

We'd done our workout thoroughly, one muscle group after another, and we'd finished up with stretching exercises on the side of the pool. I can now bend better than I've been able to do in years—I can even run! Sheila, who's a serious swimmer and body-building type, one of the rare classmates with a Real Waist, was floating peacefully as I paddled slowly toward the ladder, not wanting the time to end. I had said something earlier about my inability to float. She flipped over and stopped me and said, "Here, let's try something."

In the shallow end, she made me lie back and, with the gentlest of touches under my neck and hips, she persuaded my clumsy sinkable body to float, telling me how to breathe to balance the weight of solid muscle and bone. I didn't float well; I needed more time to tell arms and legs and lungs how to work together. But I did float a little, as with small expert touches she helped the water take and support me. She said, "I can't bear to have anyone *not* know how peaceful it feels, just to float."

Now, how can I tell her this?

I could use the Styrofoam supports and float more easily, more certainly, than I could simply with water and her touch. But Styrofoam would not reach into the hard-knotted places in my soul and untangle them, as her touch did. Styrofoam may support, but it does not minister. There is ministry in loving touch, however casual and apparently unimportant. Sheila's hands ministered to me in her desire that I should know this particular joy of floating. And my joy came not from floating, but from the strange sensation of accepting her loving ministry, in its gentleness and unobtrusiveness and utter unself-consciousness. This is new, this is different. This is love.

"Practice random acts of kindness and acts of senseless beauty." You don't know—you can't know!—what a smile given to a stranger in the street might do. They say a butterfly flaps its wings in Peking and starts a chinook in Edmonton. I don't know. Random acts of kindness—at least there's no question of reward or benefit or praise. And what's senseless beauty? Our movements in the pool get us nowhere—in fact, that's the point, working hard without apparent progress. But beauty somehow emerges.

I'm slow to warm to this business of becoming a physical person; I've had so little practice, and I've started terribly late. I think we can write off my ever competing in the Olympics. But at the same time I'm discovering things about my physical self that I hadn't been aware of, and mostly it's a very positive process. I'm in better shape than I have any right to be, for someone who's left this so long, and my motor memory and flexibility are starting to come along.

The soul too has its exercises, and the spirit sculls hard against the current, working through water. For some, that means moving from irresponsibility toward discipline, from selfishness toward loving responsibility, from torpor toward action, from arrogance toward humility, from anger toward forgiveness. For others, going against the current may mean moving from pain and constraint, hard labor and oppression, toward playfulness, freedom, authority, authenticity, courage. There's paradox, again, but with the sound of laughter somewhere behind it, and perhaps some splashing.

Repentance is a matter of working strongly against resistance, but low-impact seems to do at least as much good to get rid of the flab as the rough stuff. Tearing at your own flesh won't do it. And you can start late. After all, we've been told that if we start late—even toward the end of the day—we'll still get our pay. In the end, there will be that gentle touch under neck and hips, sustaining us as we float in Love.

It's neat, though, that this work of body and soul can in fact involve silliness as well as hard work—Styrofoam floats and whoops and hollers in the water. It's pure joy when work unites with play. It's good to be reminded that the foolishness of God is greater than the wisdom of man, the weakness of God greater than the strength of man. Sometimes we're meant to remember that we are, in fact, only silly children splashing in the water, vulnerable, playful, profoundly in need of tenderness and gentle hands-on care.

How random; how piebald; how silly. How loving.

Lot's Wife

There's no doubt that Elaine had it *very* rough. All through her childhood, her mother was seriously depressed; when Elaine was sent away to a relative because her mother couldn't cope, the relative was abusive. She married; the marriage fell apart, and she was left to bring up two kids on no money. The daughter developed an eating disorder. The boy got into bad company. Elaine, meanwhile, struggled to make a career for herself as a realtor, operating at stress levels that would stun a moose. And nonetheless, while all this was going on, she managed to be a very good mother, a fine colleague and hard worker, a compassionate and concerned person, a good friend—a real blessing. She did make it. Her kids turned out well; she found herself, in her fifties, with a secure career, a sufficient income (by her standards, which aren't high), friends, a good life.

And then it all started to change. . . . Her mother died, and Elaine went for counseling and began to unbury and examine the past, much of which had been really, truly horrible. I would have expected a period of pain and struggle as she looked into her past, and then healing and peace as she began to come to terms with it. But in fact she seemed to implode.

Of course we all have to struggle with anger sometimes. We may have long-term resentments that come hopping after us, leaping up onto our backs however often we try to shrug them off and set them down again. The ability truly to forgive comes in God's good time, and sometimes it seems to take forever.

And we all have our causes in which we KNOW we're RIGHT and are angry at those who think otherwise and who are clearly, wrong, *wrong*, WRONG. We can't seem to get past our anger at their inability to understand and accept our self-evident rightness.

But there is also the real and reasonable anger that any normal, healthy mortal feels when life slaps him- or herself upside the head once too often, for no good apparent reason. Life is sometimes neither kind nor fair. In fact, it can be hell. Elaine's anger was perfectly reasonable, given what she'd gone through. The question was: how was she going to handle it?

Once she realized that she had a right to be angry about the way her life had gone, Elaine faced a choice—a fork in the road. One path would lead her through wilderness country—through the country where our only real company can be God. On that journey, we learn (usually the very hard way!) to accept ourselves and others, to come to terms with the past, to find ways to forgive— not for our enemy's sake, but for our own. We learn to give over judgment to God, accepting that we can never know the truth, not really. We learn to accept that God loves even those who hurt us so badly. We learn to trust God to sort it all out and to do real justice in the end, because in the end only God knows what the truth really is. With that hard journey finished, we can set anger (even just and reasonable anger!) down and walk on, lightened of the burden of it. That path is hard, but it does bring us out into a place of light and life and deep healing.

Elaine took the other road. She got just enough psychotherapy to make everything worse—to justify her deep and abiding resentment. Life had given her too much shit, and she had no intention of accepting any shit from anyone else ever again, thank you very much. Her therapist told her to "own" her anger; instead, it began to own her. She became more and more irritable and suspicious, quick to snap, remote, easily offended, good at holding grudges. Insofar as she had a spiritual life at all, it seemed mostly to consist of her blaming her church for what had happened to her. She had nothing but contempt for the hard path toward forgiveness. It was all just more Christian shit, and she wasn't going to take any of that, remember? We had been on good terms, but I began to dread running into her as she seemed to get smaller, angrier, and more bitter every time I saw her, quick to jump on my failings and bully me, swift to pounce and find fault. She seemed pickled in resentment, like a cucumber in brine.

Like salt, anger is *clean*. Looking back, I think I can understand why Elaine chose it over forgiveness. She always was an idealist, a perfectionist, not one to compromise her standards; and forgiveness always does involve some compromise, a willingness not to press for pure justice. She seemed to see forgiveness as a sort of wussiness, a failure in courage. Her anger made her feel right with herself; it gave her energy, charged her up, revved her engine. She was almost like an athlete in training with her anger. It was her achievement, something she could be proud of. She could glory in its purity, its strength, its honor, its vigor and aliveness. It made her feel whole and right. She lived in her past, hanging on to it proudly, Lot's wife, looking back, transformed into a pillar of salt.

Salt is antiseptic. It cleanses. It does this by drawing the fluid out of living cells and thereby killing them. Sow the earth with salt and it will grow nothing; that is, I suppose, a sort of purity. . . . So too anger feels purifying. Anger *knows*, while love is muddled and uncertain and full of self-doubt. Anger is satisfactorily simple, deeply pleasing in its straightforwardness, energetic and plain, and really very easy, compared to love, which is none of these things. Love is messy; love is sloppy and complex; love has no easy answers. Love means accepting our own imperfections and forgiving others their failures, seeing them as fully human and coming to grips with our own (God help us!) humanity.

I do miss the old Elaine; I had been fond of her. But I can't love salt. Salt doesn't want to be loved. It wants to be salt. How can you hug Lot's wife after her transformation? Who wants to sit over tea and natter with her? She is in a world apart from hugging and tea. She stands transfixed in her purity, her clear simplicity, blindingly white, straight and upright and bending not at all, firmly grounded, forever looking over her shoulder with her eyes forever fixed on what she *knows* really matters.

The Thing
With Twigs

Last night, unable to get home for the snow, I arranged to stay with friends in town. On my way over to their house I drove along the river parkway through a still, serene landscape, full of mystery and diffused light. Turning south, away from the river, I found myself with a faceful of beauty: a snow-filled sky made the softest gray-gold by the city's reflected light, and against it, a scattered array of trees, bare, upstanding, and suddenly glorious.

I fell in love with the greenery of woods when I was a child; it was a little longer before I fell in love with the beauty of bare trees. It was (I remember) March, the year I turned sixteen, and the Vermont sky was that perfectly clear and soft cyan blue that New England skies can reach at the very instant that winter swings around in the direction of spring. The trees were elms. That much I remember. I remember being ambushed by the moment—by the sturdy patience of the boles, slender and strong, and the phenomenal intricacy, the delicacy, of the crowns, thousands of twigs, each alive, but with life on hold for the duration. Ever since that moment, winter trees have always, to me, symbolized waiting and promise.

I had been reflecting earlier on promise and endurance—how we wait through these seasons of make-do or dryness, of patience and not-knowing, or of hardship and pain, as trees wait through the winter. But unlike trees, our seasons are not regular. We don't know when summer will come—maybe tomorrow, maybe next year, maybe in the Life to Come. We do have the promise of joy, and we can wait in faith and trust for the promise to be fulfilled, but we're not given a definite delivery date.

And the path ahead may be no fun at all. God's purpose for us is deeply loving, but that doesn't mean life is necessarily going to be easy. There are those accidents of nature, or those consequences of our own or others' choices for ill instead of good, that can suddenly or slowly break us to bits and face us with rebuilding our lives with God's help, a painful process. Life's frequently Interesting, sometimes much too Interesting.

But in thinking of trees, I wasn't considering catastrophes; I was thinking more of the dailiness of things and how sometimes life does seem to be endlessly leafless. Balancing hope and endurance is not an easy business. On one hand, we're called to trust that God has our best interests very much in mind, and to set anxiety aside and simply get on with the business of living, as the lilies live without fretting much about the morrow. On the other hand, as the Prophet said, "Trust in God, and keep your camel tied." Nobody said we were supposed to be stupid. Prudence is one of the Seven Cardinal Virtues. So: how do we live in Hope without necessarily getting our hopes up?

I found a way of thinking about this in C. S. Lewis (big surprise!) in a passage from the *Screwtape Letters*. The experienced demon Screwtape tells his nephew Wormwood to keep his patient firmly focused on the future. Whether the patient is smug about his prospects or fearful doesn't much matter; either state is desirable, from damnation's point of view. "The Enemy"—God—wants us to live in the Now and in the Life to Come, but not much in the Future. Enough to manage life, yes—to plan how to pay the taxes, to organize tomorrow's work, which are (Lewis notes) *today's* tasks for tomorrow. But to dwell in the future, whether hopefully or fearfully, to seek to shape or control Today for the sake of Tomorrow, is to lose the present. And it's in the present, Lewis says, that we operate as freely as God does: the present is when our time touches Eternity. In it, we should be "obeying the present voice of conscience, bearing the present cross, receiving the present grace, giving thanks for the present pleasure."

All this had been stewing quietly on the back burner of my mind, sending up the occasional burping bubble, through the last days, underneath the scurry of busyness and artificial crises and juggling this and that. I could accept it all intellectually, but my senses and spirit were still grudging. Okay, I'll buy the idea, but it doesn't seem like much fun . . .

But then somehow it all came together as I turned south from the parkway and saw, upstanding against the glowing sky, those trees, not just in patient enduring bareness, but in such beauty that the sight whomped the breath right out of me.

Patience and endurance don't have to be plain-faced virtues. Fulfillment isn't the only thing with beauty; the bare tree in winter is as full of that quality as the deepest-leaved forest. It's merely a matter of being open to *this* beauty instead of comparing it to *that* beauty and finding it wanting.

Hope doesn't mean counting on one's dreams coming true. Hope means being willing to entertain dreams in the first place— but without being so in love with them as to give up the present beauty in hopes of something better. Hope is to dream, but to dream as lightly as a cat sleeps, without losing *this* moment. Hope is to front the past with courage: *that* happened, it may happen again, but if it does, God will get me through it. Hope is to let God, not your own wants and fears, own the future and your soul.

Hope steps into, through, and out the other side of bare belief, and trusts love to make good on its promise.

Part Four

Mud Season (2)

The Surviving Thing

I set the last stitch to the last leaf in the central motif, flipped
the hoop over, tied off the crewel yarn, slipped it under the
stitches on the back to make a neat finish, snipped the yarn, and
popped the thing out of the hoop. It's the first piece of crewel embroidery I've ever done explicitly for myself—a wreath, predomi-
nantly in roses and green—and it turned out very well. When I can
afford, I'll have it framed and hang it in my dining room, over the
oak sideboard. Until then, it's draped over the back of the wicker
sofa in the living room, where I can admire it when I pass.

The vast majority of humanity will leave no trace of its existence on the face of this earth, except (of course) for the children
we bring to birth and raise. These embroideries of mine may or
may not survive. This writing of mine may or may not still exist.
The work I do professionally, because it is largely governmental,
will indeed be in some archive somewhere, but likely without
readers. And it will not be known to be mine, and it isn't, in fact,

truly mine, of me—just something I do for a living, as well as I can, but without vocation or investment.

"The monuments rise, the monuments fall, the papers are signed and fall into chaff," Malvina Reynolds wrote in a mournful little song. And this could be a counsel of despair: what's the point of our lives if, in a hundred years or so, nobody will remember? If our work only survives by accident, or not at all? I see a sampler hung on a wall, the work of a young girl who patiently set these tiny, careful stitches some two hundred years ago—but those small fingers are long dust, as the fingers that touch this keyboard will be, in a few years' time. Lord only knows who that child truly was. Only a few Napoleons will be remembered for their great achievements or monstrosities.

I don't know if it's self-comforting illusion to believe so strongly that there is a something that survives—an essence, like a flavor of ourselves, a you-ness of you, a me-ness of me, as the molecule limonene is the lemon-ness of lemon and fills the room with its fragrance when you scrape a lemon's rind. Maybe I'm fooling myself if I believe that this essence-of-me came from somewhere and is going to somewhere—that this life is part of its journey, but not *all* of its journey. The mind can be a greatly self-deluding thing, after all. It's in my interest to believe that I have a soul, and that it is immortal, because what's the alternative? That I may be remembered for my embroideries? And what if they don't survive? Am I to believe that I am only here to manufacture children and pass on my genes? And what if my children are childless? Or must I go down to the grave and be nothing? Oddly, I can accept this latter without regret. I just don't think it's true.

But I can't know for sure, because only in the gospel of John did any mere mortal cross the River—*really* cross it, not wade in it briefly—and come back, and John doesn't tell us what Lazarus saw. I do, however, know something on a purely practical level: this life does, in fact, seem to go better if I assume that I do have a soul, and that it's going to be around when this middle-aged unlovely body of mine finally kicks the can.

If I believe, as I do believe, that I am answerable to my Creator for what I have made of this essence-of-me, then it behooves me to sit up right smartly and pay serious attention to the gospels. Christ told us what the standard was—you shall love the Lord your God with all your heart and soul and mind and strength, and you shall love your neighbor as yourself. That's the specification my soul has got to meet. I will not meet it perfectly; I know that. I cannot *make* myself be good; I can only do what I can do—which is usually rather more than I *think* I can do, or really want to do—and accept that the rest is going to need forgiveness. Only Christ himself was Light clear through; the rest of us are a mixture.

But when I take this position, so much that scrambles up ordinary day-to-day life seems to become irrelevant and silly—materialism, for example, or nursing grudges, or grabbing precedence, or getting my own way. (Mind you, I'm still very fond of the latter.) And that does simplify the process of becoming perfect—although not in the sense that most people think of when they hear that word.

I am called to be the most of what God gave me to be—to grow to my fullest extent in this life. That doesn't mean happy self-indulgence, though; it means the opposite. To bear the most fruit, an apple tree needs careful pruning. To run at her top speed and form, an athlete needs diligence and hard practice and the capacity to endure and to push on to the limits. Soul-making is more like that than it is like "discovering the inner child," although self-knowledge and self-discovery are a part of the process—just as an athlete needs to know her body before she plans her training.

It is not a process for the lazy. Any bringing-to-birth requires pain and hard work, the soul as well. The pain is the pain of dawning consciousness, of increasing awareness. The work is struggling against sloth and fearfulness and our own limits, as a moth has to struggle free of its chrysalis or a brand-new chick has to fight free of its shell. It's like the clearing of land for a field: fierce and wholesome work, ongoing, but with a certain satisfaction that has nothing to do with ego and everything to do with seeing real results.

But God already knows what the results could be. God knows us all in all, and will bring us to know ourselves all in all—now there's a scary thought. . . .

Another embroidery fills the hoop now, a small piece, for a friend—totally different, compact in form and densely worked in the richest jewel colors I could find. I enjoy setting the stitches, packing them close to make a textured surface, letting my mind wander and explore as my yarn makes its drum sound through the taut cloth. In a few days I'll set the last stitch to this one, tie off the yarn, and slip it under the stitches on the back to make a neat finish, pop it out of the hoop, and send it off—and the dear Lord knows where it will fetch up in a hundred years' time.

Mud Season (2)

In a hundred years' time, long after this life has set the last stitch in me and popped me out of the hoop, I will (I suspect) have only just begun to learn what lies on the other side of the River. But one thing I know, to the bottom of my being: that land will be filled with love.

Sneaky Joys

For three days now, it's thawed: rising temperatures at first, and now rain. Fog rises from the snowbanks and the landscape is much the uglier for the change: roadside heaps of slush slouching away into grit piles, all sorts of things exposed that had been decently buried for the duration. Still, the thaw does at least presage the end of winter. We're past the worst now; the thaw declares it. If this keeps up for a day or two more, we might even be snowless. Not bad, for March.

The sidewalks are, however, something of a problem: water over ice, *not* entertaining. So when I was walking home with my groceries from the store yesterday, I stuck to a back street and walked on the road. The alternative—going ass over teakettle on the sidewalks—could be both painful and undignified. I had the back street to myself, which is just as well, because grownups of my mature (ha!) age are not supposed to do what I was doing. At least, not where other grownups can see them.

The phenomenon is simple enough: in a thaw, the underside

of an ice deposit tends to melt before the topmost layer, leaving the top brittle. There's an odd whitish, lacy look to underrotted ice, a look that just begs a person to crack the ice with her boot heel. The ice makes such satisfying noises: good loud popping snaps when it's a large thickish sheet of ice over a shallow puddle; a finely crackling sound when it's the lacy ice-edge next to the pavement.

If you walk very slowly and ruminatively, as though you were thinking Large Important Thoughts, people might not notice that you aren't really walking in a straight line, and they might not hear what you're doing. They might not think of you as an overgrown six-year-old. (Then again, they might be jealous. . . .)

It's one of those idiot things like popping bubble wrap; you really don't want to admit how much fun it is. And besides, once you've busted up all the ice in the driveway, or popped all the bubbles in the sheet of bubble wrap, your kids find out, and they give you That Look—half "Motherrrr, how *could* you be so childish?" and half "Ma, you didn't leave us any!"

It did strike me—I had to have some justification for ice-bashing!—that there are parallels between what happens to ice in a thaw and to what happens to us after we've accepted that God is going to do a better job of running our lives than we can. If you can see your sense of wrongness or brokenness or sinfulness as being like an old ice deposit, left by life's winters in your past, then grace can act like a gentle, almost imperceptible thaw. The change is initially subsurface; the surface seems untouched, unchanged—in fact, you likely haven't the slightest idea of the changes going on right down there at the bottom. But as the underside thaws, the surface begins to take on a fragility, an instability, a vulnerability—and perhaps it gets uglier for a while, too. Then, when the change has slowly worked its way up from the bottom, the top can break easily.

If we try to deal with our brokenness the tough way—on our own without getting God into it—the process is more like pounding at old ice with a spade or chopper: very hard work for little effect, nothing really more than roughening the surface to make it more manageable—and no budging the mass underneath, most discouraging. And often we're trying consciously to "manage" our brokenness as though it were a disobedient child, usually for all the wrong reasons. But grace invited can do the same work, apparently without effort. The difference is that now, when we step childlike on the same ice—the ice we couldn't budge by our own adult efforts—it breaks with a minimum of effort. And with a deeply soul-satisfying snap.

Tomorrow, of course, it's supposed to freeze; and then we'll be back in winter again for a while. We mostly find salvation regularly and lose it again; where did I leave it last? On top of the refrigerator, or on the front hall windowsill? Maybe for some people finding God is an all-or-nothing one-time business, but for me and the people I know, it's much more like Canada at the end of winter: cycles of thaw and freeze, apparent progress and backsliding—until by Easter (more or less!) the lengthening days have done their work, and the ice is gone from the land, and there is the promise of greenness.

Charlie's Knot

My friend Charlie is trying to sort out her recently ended marriage. We spend an enormous amount of time patiently combing through the strands—or rather, trying to figure out which strands are which, because at the moment it all looks like one big hellacious knot. I don't know Charlie's ex, so I can't assess his side of things. I do know Charlie pretty well, and she gives every evidence of being a genuinely good and loving person. From the outside, on the basis of my limited and lopsided evidence, I'd say that, objectively speaking, there's a very good chance that Charlie has been making like a doormat and that her ex was (is) selfish and immature, a screwed-up and deeply angry person—but who am I to say?

Who is Charlie to say, either? None of us can judge a situation while we're in it, and she's too freshly out of it to have any real grip on what happened. Sometimes this sort of postgame failure analysis is easy and straightforward: somebody made a not too serious mistake and is sorry, and then forgiveness is very easy. Or somebody made a not too serious mistake and refuses to say sorry, and we have the sense and maturity to shrug and move on. Or somebody committed a real wrong but wants to acknowledge it, perhaps make restitution, certainly be reconciled, and then forgiveness is an act of joy. Or someone committed a real wrong and shows every sign of wanting to walk away from the logical consequences, which is a Problem because, as Santayana wisely observed, "Those who cannot remember the past are condemned to repeat it."

And then there are the hard cases. The sometimes devastating consequences of physics, biology, or real Evil can be phenomenally tough to forgive, and I'm not sure how anyone deals with that—and especially with Evil. I don't know if any human being can truly forgive Real Big Evil; I think we're too small for that. All we can do, I suspect, is to refuse to join it by declining to act in its ways.

More commonly, however, we're faced with knots: confused, uncertain situations, like the one Charlie faces: "he said/she said," "she did/he made her do"—situations in which very little is clearcut and there's something to be said for both sides. Which of us truly understands the other person's motive, much less our own? Who are we to judge?

I can't say to Charlie, "Simply forgive." First, forgiveness is rarely simple. For starters, it often takes a very long time to figure out whether, in fact, real forgiveness is called for—whether there's something that really does need forgiving, objectively speaking; and if so, what it is. Sometimes, in fact, that knowledge comes only *after* the forgiveness itself—that is, first we forgive; then we finally figure out what happened.

Second, for Big Deep Hurt, which Charlie is struggling with, the forgiving process is more like mourning than anything else; it's a process, a regular dance of repeated figures, each time letting go a little more, allowing the beloved/the grievance to slip slowly away, clutching it back, letting it go again. After all, she really did love the guy for a very long time, and it's not so easy to stop.

Third, I have no idea what forgiveness might mean under these circumstances. Forgiveness can come to different endings, embracing or letting go: the arms opening in the joy of reconciliation, or a door gently but finally closing in the sadness of parting.

And fourth and most importantly: I don't know what the process is going to do for Charlie's soul, but it could be quite a lot, and for that reason, I don't think it would be wise for her to skimp the process. She's not one to hold a grudge and I can't see her wallowing in the Sin of Anger; there's not a self-righteous or judgmental bone in Charlie's tired, patient, forbearing body. She's a genuinely loving person. Others I can think of need a good solid whack upside the skull and a reminder that "righteous anger is so often just self-righteousness"—but not Charlie. She is, in fact, a little too quick to go for cheap forgiveness—the sort that patches over real pain instead of properly dealing with it.

It could be that God will make Charlie do this forgiveness business the long, slow, painful, thorough way, because that's a marvelous way of making a person develop her spiritual leg muscles. Wouldn't be the first time.

But poor Charlie . . . She's finding it very hard. Anger and hurt and grief keep jumping her from behind. She can't forgive herself for not forgiving. It hasn't really occurred to Charlie yet that she too is human—that her own soul is just as tangled as the knot she's struggling with. When she can finally let go of the knot of her marriage and start trying to understand her own inner tangled-ness—accepting that, as a mere Miserable Offender, she can't understand all this and do the necessary forgiving work on her own—then her fingers will relax and she will be able to loosen her grip on the knot she's clutching. And *then* God can quietly nip in and sneak the knot away for God to work on Godself.

I strongly suspect that eventually she'll have to toss the whole impossible tangle over her shoulder, muttering, "Okay, Lord, I give up. I can't do this. Your turn!" Which may be the best definition of forgiveness of all. In God's hand and in God's good time, and not a minute before—and this can take years!—the knot gently untangles itself and its strands finally lie plain and clear for any eye to see.

In time, I think Charlie will have to let the wrong, whatever it is, stand on its own, and she will simply step past it, trusting that in the end it will become something she can finally see clearly. That would be very like Charlie. And it would be very like forgiveness.

But what matters most in all this is the direction Charlie's soul is taking. She *wants* to forgive, to acknowledge her own strands in the knot, to come to terms with her own internal tangle, to let it go to God. Her god in all this is God, not the knot; she does not worship her wrongs, whatever they are. She is willing to forgive, if not yet able. And that, I think, is all that God really asks. The rest will follow.

And a Time for Every Purpose Under Heaven

They want the report out on Earth Day, for God's sake, printed and bound and ready for distribution. It's too big, too unwieldy, the client is still moving text around and editing in page proofs, what about indexing? You can't index a five-hundred-page highly technical document in a week, in two official languages yet, because this is federal government stuff and it has to be in English and French. And then there's production. . . . But we're not allowed to use the I-word—"impossible." We're professionals. We get it done somehow, at whatever cost to ourselves. That's what the client expects—the client, who knows nothing of the process and has very little idea of what is and isn't possible. Oy.

So we were standing out in the hallway by the elevator, feeling slightly panicky, and someone muttered the unofficial company motto: "Give us one loaf, half a fish, and fifteen minutes." Someone else reminded us of the definition of a bureaucrat: a person who would tell a committee of nine women to produce a baby in one month. And I remembered the motto I had developed over ten years' experience as a freelance editor:

You cannot hurry a book, a pregnancy,
or a hard-boiled egg.

There is a rhythm to book production. Steps fall in a certain order: first draft, major revisions, editing, minor revisions (several times), final copy edit/proofread, page proofs, final proofread and corrections, index, print run, binding (of course that's a simplified version, but). The stages fall into this order for very good reasons, and in good publishing houses a reasonable amount of time is allotted to each step, so that the editing and copy editing are done thoroughly before the manuscript is laid out in page proofs. (That's where it appears in proper printed-page format.)

But while most of our clients are very reasonable people, some want to drive the process faster. They want to take final laid-out text into the meeting with the boss, to impress him or her, and they want it *now*. They want the first set of revisions by Tuesday, because that's the boss's birthday, regardless of what work is involved. They want to plunge into production before they've taken the time to finalize the manuscript. Without knowing anything about the steps, or why the process is as it is, they have already decided that it should go exactly as they want it to, when they want it to. And so we're plunged from crisis to crisis, working under extreme pressure through weekends—because they will not let the process unfold the way it should. A lot of our work turns out to be wasted, or inefficiently done, because the process gets hopelessly gummed up by the rush.

But that's not how a good process unfolds. Healthily growing things take their time and cannot be rushed. You cannot tell a rose to hurry it up. You can't tell a heart to be mended by Friday. If you're coming up from the depths, it's going to take years, not months. You cannot *truly* forgive until the time comes for forgiveness, hard as you may try. You cannot tell a maple to reach a hundred feet by the year 2000, or else. Some things just take their own sweet time.

It goes both ways. You also cannot put the child on hold until you get around to her; by the time you're ready, she'll be grown—just as, in a healthy birth, she pushed her way into the world at her own rate, regardless of whether or not you were ready for her arrival. Lilac season only lasts a couple of weeks. Some things go at their own precipitous rate, regardless of your convenience. What was that old line? "Under precisely controlled laboratory conditions, living things will do what they damned well please."

Goes for God, too. Once we give up the notion of trying to run our own lives and turn them over to our Abba, Abba will act in Abba's own good time, and if we have a problem with that, it's *our* problem. The healing and grace will come in due course, and it's useless to try to speed the process up, or to stop it. The gifts we so passionately desire will come when we're ready for them, not before—and we usually aren't ready nearly as soon as we think we are. Or they may come *before* we think we're ready, because Abba has decided that today's the day—got a problem with that?

Wanting things in *our* time is simply another aspect of our own willful desire to have it our way: "My will, not Thy will." And we may get what we thought we wanted, but the chances are good it won't do for us what we wanted it to do. (What's the old line, "Be careful what you pray for—you may get it"?) The report we're scrambling to get out now will be full of problems that should have been caught; it won't be the work it should be, and that will leave it open to criticism. The quick fix comes unglued very quickly. The easy waters that looked so tempting turn out to be shoal and full of sandbanks.

Instead, we have to learn to possess our souls in patience, while being ready to accept what God wants us to have when God wants to give it to us—which means living in the tension of hope, not an easy place to be (which is why so few people manage it, and I speak as one who knows!).

But all things come in God's good time, to those who put their trust in God. For to everything there is a season, and a time for every purpose under heaven.

Branta canadensis

The geese are back.

The landscape's still just coming out of Mud Season—there's the odd haze or patch of green amid the ochers and straw-browns and gray-greens of the cedars. The tips of the twigs thicken as the buds come along. Another week will make a huge difference. Another week, and it may actually be green around here.

But for now, optimism is in the geese. They take a break from the long flight north, settling to rest and feed on the flooded land alongside the big river to the north of town. And then, when they're ready for the next stage, they take off in their hundreds— big, clumsy birds with their unmistakably thick and rounded bodies, breaking into smaller groups and painstakingly forming the long Vs that gladden and half break the heart to watch.

They have come so far, and they have so far to go, and they're working so hard in the process. They are not like hawks and gulls, riding the air without apparent effort, as though they'd been hatched already airborne. Instead, the geese seem to have to pound at the air with their wings to keep going. It's all very systematic and methodical, competent but not graceful, and it looks like extremely hard work.

But something takes them north, just as something took them south last fall, and that something has to do with their nature and the pattern of their lives. They breed in the great northern marshes, where their goslings are safe from predators; and they summer in the south because there's no food here to sustain them through the long winters. It all makes a certain cockeyed biological sense—but oh, the work it takes!

We'd all like to be born again, to be converted without apparent effort—to be picked up by God's hand and set down exactly where and as we should be—abracadabra (poof!) problems solved, relationships restored, hurts healed, bad habits broken. But in fact we're more like the geese painstakingly beating our way home, one stage at a time.

If we have sense, we'll travel together: a lone goose is a dead goose. We need company on the Journey. But it is a journey, and the journeying itself matters very much; it isn't merely a means to the end, but a necessary process. It's in the course of beating our way slowly home that we make our souls—create who it is that we will give back to our Creator when we come before God's judgment. If we're wise, we listen both to the Holy Spirit, a magnet within us drawing us toward that greatest Source, and to the other geese—our companions, our tradition (remembering, though, that geese are geese, not God).

The paths we take are known. There is no single path for the geese. Can you imagine them in their millions trying to follow a single corridor north or south? Likewise, there are many paths toward the same fulfillment, but always they seem to have certain common features. When we read what's left by those who went before us—the psalmist, the saints and mystics—we hear, in language piquantly different from ours, the same landscape described that we're passing through now. And that's comforting, because it says that we are indeed on course: "Aha!—*that's* what *this* bend in the river is!"

Probably to the geese—I'm not a wildlife biologist—the landscape apparently stays uniformly at the same stage in late Mud Season as they pass through it; the green follows them as they move slowly northward, on the leading edge of spring. So to us, our progress may seem nonapparent: the scenery really doesn't look much greener than it did yesterday. There has been no great transforming miracle.

Only the landscape *is* different. We've come another piece, into a new stretch of country. Love doesn't follow us, as the new green follows the geese; it's there already, if we could only see it, forever overtaking us, surrounding us, preceding us on our long road.

Home lies at the end. Once there, we can rest. And we will never have to journey back again.

And by Its Nature Grow

I was in a hurry to get home and get my bread started, so after some hesitation I risked taking the shortcut. At this time of year, the path between the mall and the road near my house can be impassable. It's deeply rutted and has to cross a ditch, and right now the thaw is on full tilt, the frost coming up slowly from the depths. The creek's as full as it ever gets, and up to the northwest the big river spreads out almost to the road's edge, flooding people's basements. The land's soft and sodden, full of water as a dishrag, as winter washes out down through the soil, filling the water table to overflowing.

So the path might be too wet to be usable at all, and maybe I'd have to get home by a longer road—but it was worth a try. I got over the ditch using the bits of board that people (who?) leave by it, for bridge-making purposes. The next bit involved tricky stepping through the sloughy bits, hopping from one firm hummock to another. But I managed to get across the worst mud and onto higher, drier ground without even seriously splashing my sneakers. And then I stood and caught my breath, because there was the sound again. . . .

The path is always full of quiet noise, every time I go there. It's too early for the buzzing, soughing noises of high summer, when the fields are full of underlife. But even so, the bit of wind stirring last year's high grass made the softest of shushing noise, gentle and light as a fingertip on bare skin.

It was not, however, a restful sound, more a sound of Things Brewing. It was that quietness which is in fact an intensity; a stillness not of rest but of energy kept in check, until the moment comes. The place felt full of a Something as intensely alive as a cat mousing. We are now poised on the cusp, waiting for it to happen. And the "it" is a newness of life, a bursting forth.

Of course the life was there all along, through the harsh depths just ending; it rested quiet until conditions were right. But now life's on the move again. And life will not be stopped. It must, in its very nature, simply grow.

Hope's slow, sometimes, just as year by year we have the slow receding of frost from the soil, leaving it this soft. But once hope gets a foothold, a little warmth, some promise, it *will*, in its very nature, simply grow. Once the Spirit gets one tendril in a person's heart, the Spirit will persist, insist, demand, to keep on growing and becoming. That's the Spirit's nature, hardwired, as these plants and trees are predetermined to leaf out just as soon as conditions allow.

The Spirit may be quiet sometimes, feeling almost absent, or may pound like a shaken heart, or rush like a creek in spate, or simply float slowly upward into consciousness, as the frost heaves out of the soil now. But it nudges and wriggles us lifeward and Godward, as surely as this season turns—as long as we consent. Because, unlike the trees, we *can* say no to life. Grace is only inevitable if we accept it.

A few more weeks and the ground here will be dry, and this place will be the green that refreshes the eye and soul. The birds and bugs will be about their birdly and bugly business. A few more weeks and the world beneath this now dry grass will be crawling, buzzing, sensing, tasting, feeling, dividing, breeding, bursting forth with growth, full of pain and pleasure. Already the life's starting, although I can't see it yet, as plant cells ready themselves to divide and grow and overwintering larvae move toward metamorphosis.

A few more weeks. Until then, even though it all seems so muddy and lifeless in this interseason between winter and spring, there will be that quiet underwhisper, like the soft hissing of the grass in the thin but strengthening April sun this morning, telling your heart simply to await God's time. For joy will indeed come in the morning.

The Cedar Bog

I'm hoping Amy will let me take her out for a walk, next time she's visiting. She's the young daughter of a friend of mine, and she's taking an increasing interest in photography—the real stuff. She's a city kid (suburban, actually), but she's starting to taste the delights of walking around actually *looking* at the countryside, up close, with a camera in hand. I used to do that once, when I wasn't much older than she is now, and I still remember the fascination.

There's one particular patch I want to take her to see, if she's willing. I don't know if she'll find it as intriguing as I do. Maybe she'll just see it as an unpleasant mess. It's a bit of cedar swamp, next to the road west of my house. Every time I walk past it I'm entranced. It has, for reasons I don't entirely fathom, a remarkable richness to it—the cedars themselves, the twisted pole-fencing, the alders and other scrub. It's all visual texture, a good tangled, complicated, satisfying roughness to the eye. With a good basic single-lens reflex camera, black-and-white film, and her own enlarger, a photographer could get playful with this patch of cedar bog.

I don't claim the patch is beautiful in the way that (say) the Public Gardens in Halifax are beautiful; there is a deeply soul-satisfying beauty in order, ceremony, color, the mastery of art, and the cedar bog hasn't got that at all. It *is* a mess, objectively speaking; and I'm sure it breeds mosquitoes by the gazillion. Merely, if we're willing to look around with a kindly and inquisitive eye, there's usually *some* beauty to be found anywhere, however messy the anywhere is.

Good artists scan the landscape for whatever it is they can use—a thing, a sound, a bit of harmony, an image, a face, a snatch of conversation in the bank lineup, the hoot of an owl—and they take that and use it as the need dictates. Good artists trawl reality, like beachcombers looking to see what the tide fetched up. It's no big deal, just a sort of continual alertness: "Hmm, what can I do with *that?*" We talk about Rules, as in Benedictines or Cistercians; well, perhaps the Rule of creativity is simply to take notice, continually, in a disciplined and mildly objective, inquisitive sort of way, with a view toward making use of what one notices.

It *is* a Rule, though; and, like any Rule, it's there to carry you through the tough places. I cannot remember how often, during the dark times, the Rule has kept me going with its own odd momentum. Must write piece for Saturday: what's there to notice this week? The writerly reflexes kick in, to find whatever is given this time (an ant, a bit of wool, a chip of limestone) and to bring to it what I have in skill and discipline. That necessary rhythm is, for me, like the measured cadence of compline and matins and vespers.

The notice and use can be positive or negative, loving or un-.

I saw a photograph at the National Gallery a few weekends ago, of an elderly woman got up *en jeune fille,* her too made-up eyes overbright in their pouches of wrinkles, rouge on her fallen cheeks, and a cupid's bow of bright lipstick on her thinned lips, the color bleeding into the fine wrinkles surrounding her mouth. And the photographer's notice was without a shred of mercy. The photo held her up in clinical mockery, pillorying her foolishness and vanity. Nearby was a postmodern sculpture of an overweight poor woman, with hair like dry straw, in a cruelly unbecoming print dress, sitting at a kitchen table reading something junky, with a carefully sculpted doughnut on a plate by her elbow. It too was merciless. But then, cruelty is easier than compassion; it's kewler to mock than to love. There's nothing like the possession of ruthless insight to fluff up the old artistic ego. . . .

The alternative is to scan the horizon with love instead of judgment. No photographer could make that poor, absurd old woman look young and beautiful again—that would be a lie—but another photographer could perhaps touch the portrait with a certain kindness, an understanding of what might make her need to feel and dress that way. You can judge my patch of cedar swamp either as a mess or as something with its own wild beauty. It's a question of subtext: are you there to weigh the thing in judgment, looking for flaws; or to hold it in love, looking for whatever beauty may be on offer?

It seems to me that the Rule of noticing with a loving eye is a form of giving glory to God, as when Gerard Manley Hopkins delighted in "all things, counter, original, spare, strange." Looking for the God in people does not require us to be blind to them, but to be open to whatever they have of goodness. Looking at my patch of cedar swamp with an eye toward God-in-it could allow someone like Amy to bring that beauty forward. In developing her eye for that beauty, she develops her eye for God-in-things. And thereby she gives glory to God, who has made all things well.

Airplanes

(FOR ANDREW GRAHAM)

From the south-slightly-east-of-central part of the city where I'd been running errands, the sensible way home is the road that goes alongside the river, out almost to my town. The road skirts the city's airport—in fact, it goes right under the takeoff flight path, close to the end of the runway. Now and again I get *really* lucky and manage to drive past just as a jet is taking off, thundering a few hundred feet overhead. As I came out on Friday afternoon, when the airport is particularly busy, I got lucky: one plane taking off almost overhead, and other planes circling, waiting to land. Wooo!

I love airplanes—not to fly on; that's a different matter, a matter of boredom and stale air and cramped seats—but to watch. Airplanes make me smile like a little kid. I turn off the car radio to hear them thunder, and I watch them as much as I can without causing an accident. I don't know a thing about airplane lore; I can't tell a 767 from a DC-whatever. I just love watching the damn things fly, especially when they're taking off or landing. They seem to me to be so wildly optimistic. What trust! What faith!

Of course I understand the physics of flight, the "hows" and "whys." The basic principles are so simple a child can grasp them—all these vectors of thrust and drag and lift, very straightforward. But at a real deep-down level, I don't believe the physics. The fact remains: anything that weighs 300,000 pounds or so ought to fall right down out of the sky like a rock. That's just obvious common sense, isn't it?

It's also obvious common sense, isn't it, that, even if you believe in God, life will go on in the future the way it has in the past, that belief can't actually *change* anything. If we try again what we tried before and failed at, we're just going to fail again. Death and taxes, that's for sure, and Murphy's Law still hold, and you can't change human nature. There are no miracles, or nothing you can't explain as a sort of magic trick. Nothing that weighs even three pounds can stay up in the sky; how can something that weighs as much as an airplane? Nahhhh . . . no way.

But in fact airplanes don't fall out of the sky. They get up there, and they *stay* up there, and they come down neatly and nicely thousands of times for every one that screws up. Very, very rarely do they fall from the sky, and then only if something has gone horribly wrong. The secret is movement and orientation. Airplanes stay up because they thrust forward at a speed that keeps a flow of air pressing upward on the underside of their wings.

Same goes for us. When we're moving forward at an appropriate speed (a 767 doesn't fly as fast as the Concorde), we have that life under us that can keep us steady when there seems to be nothing under us but air. It's getting stuck—usually because we're too afraid to trust that God has a good grip on us—that leaves us floundering, rolling, and crashing.

Anyone who's flown a kite (another occupation to which I have been partial) knows that the crucial thing is to keep the kite's nose up so the air presses up on its underside. Same goes for us. When we keep our noses pointed in the right direction—not keeping them resolutely stuck in our own navels, not looking down them at other "inferior" people (a besetting sin of Christians in all places and times), not sniffing out other people's sins to reinforce our own unimpeachable Moral Superiority—then we feel that Wind that can raise us higher and higher and keep us steady, still tethered to this world, but soaring.

Face forward; move even when you don't feel solid ground under your feet; keep your nose pointed straight toward the Light, while staying tethered in this world (for, as the rule has it, "Takeoff is optional; landing is mandatory"). Have faith that you won't fall from the sky like a stone, that God's breath will be under you, pressing you upward, holding you in its power. Do that, and you can feel it under your wings, that Wind of God, the Spirit at active work in *this* world, lifting you high, keeping you safe and steady on your way.

The Garden

Had a chat with an unchurched commodities broker the other day. I mentioned something about my writing, and he asked enough questions to realize that I do most of my writing about God, something he clearly found absolutely lunatic. I found myself wondering what I could say to him, or to others like him, about the process we're engaged in—how to describe it? How to make any sense of it? I tend to work metaphorically, and a metaphor came to mind—I don't know if it works, but I had fun playing with it.

Consider: each of us is given a plot of ground. The nature of the ground will vary, from rich alluvial flatness to rocks and hillsides, and the size of the plot may vary a bit, although no plot is either huge or tiny. Our job as souls is to make of our plot whatever our plot allows us to make of it, given the resources we have to work with.

No two plots are the same; nor are any two gardeners. Some have more imagination or intelligence than others; some have

greater or lesser physical strength. Some have been crippled or seriously damaged and can do less, or very little (and oddly, their
lots often have a wild beauty all their own); others are merely bone
lazy, uncaring, uninterested.

But there's no point looking over at the next person and either
sniffing at his efforts or envying what she's done. Your job is to
make the best of what has been given to *you*, stretching your own
limits in the process.

It's amazing how many people think that the ideal is a green
suburban lawn, and spend much time and energy and effort trying to flatten out their bumps and valleys, planting grass where
grass shouldn't ought to be, and going into anxiety attacks (and
trotting out the toxic chemicals) over invading quack grass. Or
some people say: PETUNIAS, and not only cover their own lots with
nothing but petunias, but insist that everyone else should be growing nothing but petunias too. Petunias are *right*. Nonpetunias are
wrong.

Other people whine that they aren't gardeners, and they don't
cultivate their lots at all, barring sometimes looking out over the
mess and wringing their hands helplessly at how far it is beyond
them, and then getting back to the TV. Still others read gardening
books endlessly but without getting dirt under their fingernails.
Others rip at the soil viciously but ignorantly, stripping away the
covering vegetation, ruthlessly tearing out boulders, intent on some
radical inner vision at whatever cost to themselves or their poor
abused plots of land. Others plant a few annuals, or a tomato or
two, and hope for the best.

But there is a better way of doing this.

If you're going to make something of your plot, you're going to have to work at building up both your understanding and your back muscles, the one through exploration, the other through daily discipline. You should learn about the process—what will grow in shade, what needs full sun, what plants are hardy or tender, how to build a pool. And there's much pleasure to be had in that process.

The single most important thing is to know what you have to work with—the nature of your plot, and what can be made of it. You require an inventory, honest and accurate—no wishful thinking! If you've got a rocky hillside with a stream flowing through it, there's no point planning a vegetable garden; look at rock gardens, and the beauty they can offer, and work the flow of water through it for music and refreshment. If you have rich alluvial soil, your choices are very different. No two lots are the same. Each lot has its particular merits, its particular problems. Each has its potential for productivity or beauty.

And that beauty has no limit. Whatever is harmonious within itself, whatever shows balance and thought and real effort, is beauty: from a Zen arrangement of rocks thoughtfully placed and gravel meticulously raked and trees trained into careful carelessness; to a deep-toned perennial bed rich with peonies and iris and lupine; to an oatfield with its sweet, clear, soft, velvety green; to a carefully formal box border. Even a windswept seashore lot, where the dwarfed trees struggle among the harsh outcrops and the waves pound and roar, has the beauty of power and endurance. And there's nothing wrong with petunias—in moderation, of course.

Each plot does have some ultimate possibility—some particular beauty, some ideal form that it's capable of, and that's what we're aiming for. That is the perfection Paul speaks of. We may not reach it in this life, but it exists.

But working toward this ideal isn't easy. Any plot requires a good deal of work—of careful, thoughtful clearing, shifting a boulder here, planting a tree there, sometimes putting a crop of clover or potatoes in to condition poor soil and then plowing that crop under. Gardening is simple drudgery much of the time, but with blessed moments when you can lean on your hoe and smile, before getting back to work.

What we Christians have, we believe, is the best instructional literature, not only on how to garden, but on troubleshooting, and plant biology, and hydrogeology, and all the other resources we need to do our work in an informed way. We have One who has taught us what it is we're supposed to do, and roughly how we're supposed to do it. But he also knows that no two plots are identical (and neither are the people who cultivate them) and so does not lay down detailed hard-and-fast rules, because what's good for the rich valley bottom doesn't necessarily work for the windswept patch on the coastline.

What we have been told, in no uncertain terms, is that we will present the results of our gardening to the God who made us. That God knows perfectly well what we have been given to work with. God knows also our own history—how, for example, an early injury might affect our ability to lift, and so we've not made all of the garden that the garden itself is capable of, but we've done as well as we could, given its and our own limitations. God knows about the floods, or the fire that wiped out years of effort, or the three-year drought; He knows not just what we have to present, but how it came to be, and the struggle it required. There's forgiveness there, and understanding. This isn't a harsh and blaming business.

God breathes life and growingness into what we plant, sends the rain and the sun—and also the necessary tough times of dormancy and endurance, because many seeds need to overwinter in order to sprout, and many fruits need a touch of frost to ripen. God throws in randomness and dancing chance, for us to seize and play with. God gave us the ground, in whatever form, and the urge to make something of it—the hunger for food and beauty. God holds in God's mind the vision we're struggling toward: that ideal form that our plot could take—will take in the Life to Come, when our gardens will come to be beyond anything we could ever ask or imagine.

Part Five

Spring

The River

Just north of town the river turns toward the city, where it debouches into the larger river that will carry its waters into the St. Lawrence at Montreal. It's not huge, our river, but it's a good size—substantial, respectable. It comes from a series of pretty lakes to the southwest, forming (with a canal) a water system much used for fishing and boating. It is also the boundary between us and the metropolitan area; while crossing the bridge, we rural unsophisticates like to meditate with gently ruminative pleasure on the difference in property taxes. The river doesn't dominate the landscape—it's not like the St. Lawrence, a noticeably Great and Historically Significant River. But it's peaceably, solidly *there*, with its own character and history.

Right now, toward the end of spring runoff, the river is broad and calm; it looks placidly monumental, like Queen Victoria in old age. It seems almost static except for the odd ripple. There's hardly a hint of visible motion. But that's deceptive. In fact, you're looking at God alone knows how many tons of water, millions of cubic meters of water, all in rapid, irresistible motion, pouring north at high speed toward the river's final outfall in the very heart of the city.

Think of a river with any sort of real awareness and its sheer weight and power become overwhelming. Think of the mass of it pushing downstream—try carrying a good-sized carboy of water any distance, and then multiply that weight by several million to get any idea, as though the mind could wrap itself around such an immensity. And this is *only* a not very big river. It goes into a much larger river, the Ottawa, which in turn flows into a very large river, the St. Lawrence—and that in turn goes into the sea. The volume and mass of all this water, the power and majesty of this movement, are simply staggering.

We think of the river as Canadian property, and legally so it is: its banks and bed belong to this country, not to (say) Estonia or Peru. We share the St. Lawrence with the United States, and there is a defined and carefully surveyed boundary line running invisibly through its gray-green grubby depths. We own out to yonder from our shores, and other countries aren't allowed to catch the fish there and have to obey our laws.

But can water really be owned? Who owns the geese flying north in their Vs at this season? Water is like cats: it doesn't "do" ownership relations. This particular river system is replenished by rain from water vapor that may once have been (in fact, certainly was) part of a river in Estonia or Peru, or from offshore waters belonging to no country at all. This river's water is in equilibrium with the water vapor in the air over it, and you can no more own *that* than you can own the air itself.

Water is free. It's bound by its own regimes, inherent in its physical and chemical structure: it has its melting point, its boiling point, its partial pressure, its specific density, its peculiar structure in both the liquid and solid states. It has its own imperatives, and they are not always ours. We can, we think, control it—until it decides otherwise, without consulting us. Think of the Mississippi floods, or the Red River and Saguenay disasters, or tidal waves, or the great ice storm that left its heavy mark on these woods and forests. Water does its own thing, and if we have a problem with that, it's *our* problem.

So: if a simple smallish Canadian river is this large, this powerful, and this tenuously under our control (if we have any control at all, which is another question), whatever gave us the out-to-lunch idea that we can own and manage God?

"Oh, of course, we'd never for a minute think we *could* do that!" we'd say, with some mixture of smugness, amusement, and theological hand-flapping. Oh, but we do! Look at how we define God, characterize God, hold back God's mercy from this sinner or that, claim God for our side and deny God to the enemy, constrain God to be like this or that. It's a very human tendency.

We'd like to dress God in human clothing, like a doll, making God one of *us*, cute or vindictive, depending on our need of the moment. We'd like to turn God into a Big Daddy Boss to be placated and pleased, or someone who has to answer our logic and expectations—on trial for the Problem of Evil. We do think we own God. Look at how much time we spend telling the other person that he or she has got God all wrong.

It's something we have to be careful about—a tendency we all must be aware of and on guard against. If you think you can hold back God from some other Miserable Offender, deny God's love to someone, go look at a river and imagine stopping it in mid-flow. I don't *think* so.

The pickerel in the river can't see the river; he can only sense what water lies around him, tasting the scents from upcurrent. The duck on the river knows the river only in her limited duckly ways. The dragonflies, the cattails, the water weeds, the herons, know the river so very intimately, and so very poorly. The difference between them and us is that we claim to understand what lies around and above and under us, while these creatures merely *are*, with and in the water.

God's love, the Holy Spirit, goes where God's nature tells it to go, just as water does. It is as much in our ownership and control as is the sea. Like water, it is in and about and around us, in every fiber of our being, and we depend on it utterly without even understanding how much we need it. Our lives float in it.

We may understand this reality and be grateful and awed by it, or we may be so preoccupied with our own *me*-centric concerns that we don't notice. But God's love is still there, steady and broad as the river, quietly powerful and peaceable as the river, but of a power we cannot begin to imagine. *That* stream is big enough to float whole galaxies, whole universes, bobbing in God's Spirit as gently as a duck on the water.

Weeds Upspringing

Green has begun to invade, as the creek starts to settle down and the tips of twigs thicken, and the air is warm enough to hang laundry out again. The daffodils are just starting to bloom, the snowdrops are that particularly endearing blue, and my forsythia is forsything. And, I rejoice to see, the dandelions are coming along nicely, as is the quack grass. The wild camomile is up and running. I haven't looked for young milkweed yet, but I'm sure it's out there. And the daylilies are upspringing wherever there's a bank suited for them (which is most places around here).

With the sole exception of burdocks (I have cats), I have a strong backhanded affection for weeds. These are the plants you'll find springing up wherever the soil's been disturbed or where nothing else will grow. They colonize unfriendly habitats like graveled road shoulders and the middle of lightly used dirt roads, turned-over soil, landfill dumps—anywhere too unpromising for "nicer" less hardy plants. Once weeds have civilized the neighborhood for plant life, then the "good" plants can move in, the domesticated grasses; and they will crowd the weeds out. But for now the weeds are flourishing, getting a jump on their respectable neighbors.

It would be going much too far to say, "The kingdom of God is like a dandelion," but I still think that's better than saying, "The kingdom of God is like a prize tulip." We'd much rather think of God-stuff as being precious, not common. But think of the metaphors Jesus uses—mustard plants, rising dough—common, earthly, robust, everyday. He doesn't hold himself aloof from the weediness of things. In fact, if his fondness for the company of sinners is anything to go by, he rather likes us weeds.

We may be terribly concerned to keep faith purebred, perfect, shielded from any potential contaminants—but that's *our* desire. It's akin to our desire to keep our faith in the most beautiful possible boxes—honoring it by setting it aside from the ugly everyday. There's a very natural, normal, rather sweet tendency of human nature to want to dress up what it loves in fancy clothing and keep it spotlessly clean and away from the ordinary muckiness of things. But that too easily becomes a tendency to declare that Dolly is too special for daily use and to put her up on the closet shelf, wrapped in clean tissue paper. I seriously doubt that God prefers to be stuck in the front parlor, kept for "best" and never used, while the rest of us are out in the kitchen having fun.

You always have to worry about prize tulips—whether they could accidentally cross with some inferior lineage, what particular nutrients they require, what carefully regulated conditions they need to produce that perfect bloom. You start them in carefully sterilized potting mix, guarding the young growth carefully against blight and pests, making sure the temperature and humidity are just right, timing the light exposure to force the perfect bloom. And for what? For your own satisfaction, your knowledge of the superiority of *your* plant—not really even for your aesthetic sense, if we're honest; daylilies are prettier, at least to some eyes, if not to all.

Daylilies, meanwhile, look after themselves, finding any old spot to grow and bloom in, coming back year after year, and blooming whenever nature calls them to it. And being hardy plants, they flourish. "Consider the lilies of the field" isn't about the handsome fragrant white plants still decking the altar after Easter; it's about these casual footloose beauties. Wild camomile doesn't look to us for protection or provision; the trilliums take care of themselves, and so do the lilacs. And they bloom whether or not we care.

Is it better to think of faith as being something delicate, fragile, easily contaminated, to be protected from the vagaries of human error, or is it better to think of faith as a hardy perennial? I think the former attitude says a whole lot about human fearfulness and our desperate need to know what The Rules are. But I don't think it says anything about the sturdiness and resilience of God.

God has given us a wonderful gift, an irreplaceable gift, and here we are, trying to dress it up in prettier wrappings and remaking it to suit our own exclusivity, our desire to feel righteous and superior, and our need to control. Is this *really* trusting in God? Is this really accepting the no-strings gift of grace that Jesus died to bring us, each and every one of us, sinners most especially included (because there are no others)? I don't think so. But then,

I'm more concerned about our tendency to forget God than I am about getting this faith business right. None of us has the answers, after all, something even St. Paul admitted.

God's grace, it seems to me, is as alive as life can be, and it will outreach, outlast, outpursue, outlove us. It is around us and under our feet, before and over us, tough as the roots of wild iris, stubbornly persistent as snow-on-the-mountain, spreading exuberantly like wild violets. It is stronger and more stubborn even than human nature, rooting in crevices and cracks in the most desolate of landscapes, growing regardless and blooming.

We can choose to uproot it from our personal gardens—usually because we're in love with prize tulips!—but it wants to creep in, like quack grass. And it *will* creep in and take over, if only we will give it half a chance. Just try to stop it, once it's got a start.

Damn

(FOR BBW)

Sigh . . .

Any of the three would have done; they were all clever and persuasive and illustrated Important Things, neatly tied to Interesting Real-Life situations. Anyone could find relatable material in them, thoughtful stuff, with just the right-sized dollop of Proper Theology. There would have been good responses that kept my ego happily stroked and smoothed, and nobody could see a thing wrong with what I'd written. Except me. And God.

For, considered properly, each of the three draft pieces I wrote was really just bitchery—paying off old scores, settling accounts with people who had hurt me. I'm tolerably insightful and very good with words, so I could nicely veil what I was up to—from others, perhaps, but not from myself. Or God. So I can't use three quite tidy bits of writing, because they might be cute, but they sure as hell aren't Christian.

I repeat: Sigh.

Of course it's easier for me to look at others' failings than at my own life. My own life, to me, looks so hopelessly unmanageable, full of very real and important and (sometimes) scary lapses and wrong commissions that I cannot for the life of me seem to correct. Thinking of my soul as a house: however much I exhaust myself trying, I can't even keep the place tidy, much less clean. Much easier to visit someone else's house, running my white-gloved fingertip over the top of the doors and imagining what's shut in the hall cupboard, than to deal with the fetid mess under my own refrigerator.

I begin to realize that when the Pharisee was muttering over his list of perfections, while sneering at the tax collector over there in the corner, maybe the Pharisee wasn't being a self-righteous religious perfectionist. Maybe he was just feeling nervous. Maybe he felt that he *had* to buy God's love, because he sure as hell didn't deserve it for just being himself. If so, we're mostly with the Pharisee.

But we know at a deeper, profoundly uneasy-making level that, however we try, ultimately God can't be bought. Like it or lump it, we are all (if we have any sense) uneasily aware that God could find quite a number of holes to pick with us, if God chose to. Technically, we may believe in God's grace and peace and love, but on the whole we've usually had a lot more experience with the hole-picking process than we've had with being honestly seen and loved and accepted, just as we are, fleas and all.

Which is probably why we're so obsessed with our own and others' misdoings. We are dimly aware of God's power to judge, and we assume that God's going to be just as judgmental about us as we are about everyone in earshot. We just want to remind God that the person over there has LOTS of holes to pick, in the hope that God may get so busy with the other guy that He'll forget about us.

But then, there's eternity. . . . won't work. Not in the very long term, anyway. If God wants to pick holes, not one of us *isn't* in big, big trouble, Mother Teresa included.

Sigh.

But there is another way, and it's the way we have . . . well, belief in at some times, faith in at some times, hope often, absolute certainty rarely, because the prospect is so breathtaking that we can't wrap our human heads around it: that God has decided to give up on picking holes at all. That as He once promised never to destroy His creation, so He promises through Christ never to hold us up to a standard none of us can meet, and never to judge us by a Law that none of us can possibly keep.

We have the assurance through Christ that God does love us exactly as we are, although He doesn't always like how we behave. The worst effects of sin are, in fact, on our relationships with each other, and the effects can be horripilating. What God offers is steady, unblinking forgiveness—not blindness; forgiveness. What God wants from us in return is a simple decision: are we going to accept forgiveness or not? Because in fact we usually *do* turn away from it, either because we figure we can't possibly deserve it or because we don't want to admit that we've done anything that needs forgiving.

It's that knowledge of the Law—what God expects of me in my writing, at its and my best—that makes me look at those three pieces and think, "These won't do." There is a standard set for me in this work, and it's my job to meet it; if I miss the mark, it's my job, through my understanding of the standard and through the Holy Spirit at work in me, to *know* I've missed the mark and to do what I can to set things right again.

I can't make myself be a Perfectly Good Person, any more than I can reduce my house-mess to Martha Stewart–like Gracious Living ‹gack› ‹sputter›, although, with much effort, I can keep us all from tumbling into total squalor. I am and will always be too human, too sloppy, too quick to feel hurt, and too slow to forgive. But I *can* decide that these pieces I write are not a place for me to pay off any private scores. That's a small resolution, not too hard to keep, one that puts to death for God's sweet sake one small part of my own particular messy human nature. Those three draft pieces might be clever bits of work, and I may yet recycle the good ideas in them in less bitchy ways, but for now—no. Into the trash bin, one, two, three.

Still, they *were* neat pieces of writing . . . Sigh. Oh, well.

(Romans 8:14–25)

The Shawl

It was eighteen dollars I didn't need to spend, but I couldn't resist the colors—iridescent gold, tawny copper, magenta, and olive green, flowing like an exotic rainbow through the Somali woman's thin gray-brown hands. At that price it was almost certainly polyester, not silk, and I was probably getting ripped off. But I bought it anyway. Maybe the same corner of me that still steps over cracks in the sidewalk hoped that, by some magic, it might lend me some of the woman's slender elegance. Didn't work, of course.

Just as the Southeast Asians and the Italians before them have flowed through the city's poorer districts, vastly improving the local restaurant scene, so the East African immigrants are adding to the visual landscape. The women, like the one who was selling scarfs and shawls, are gravely graceful in their elegantly wrapped headscarfs and long dresses, fine-boned and long-limbed and large-eyed, many of them as beautiful as anything on a magazine cover. But the men are handsome too, and the children are simply stunning.

Of course there will be some problems. Some of these people will fit in and prosper; others will go wrong or fail. The city isn't totally tolerant of different racial and religious groups—is any city? There are potential areas of irritation: to this Muslim woman, seeing my bare head, arms, and legs may be as jarring as it would be for me to live in a culture where women went bare-breasted. When I looked her in the face and smiled, was I being friendly and comforting or was I intruding on her personal space and being aggressive? I don't know. We must strain their patience considerably sometimes. And sometimes they may strain ours.

It must be hard to watch your children turn away from the values that your parents inculcated in you, and begin to shift into the dominant culture. It must be hard to have trouble finding the stuff you need to cook with (although I notice some city supermarkets now carry mutton and kid, and there are *halal* stores). It must be hard to struggle with the language, the transit system, the seasons—my God, what must it be like to live with the winters here, if you're used to a subtropical climate?

Of course there are also major advantages. If you've spent years in a country in chaos and civil war, then whatever the climate, the sheer blessed peace and security of Canada must be something to be deeply, daily grateful for. This country is at the top of the list of good places to live, and with reason. But still, this woman is an exile, and to be an exile is not easy.

We too are exiles if we think about it. There is a Kingdom of God, we believe, and it has not yet come to pass on this earth. If there is a life to come, we aren't there yet. This world is not always as we want it; sometimes its values are not our values and often its selfish, uncaring, violent, greedy ways can hurt our hearts. It isn't always easy.

But for many, maybe for most people, life is exile of one sort or another. How many people do feel at ease in their lives, comfortable and happy? Some, but I don't know too many.

Maybe that's why the Babylonian captivity is such a feature of the Old Testament: to tell us that we aren't alone in feeling we don't belong here, even if there may be real advantages to being where we are, real and solid joys in our lives. The prophet, sending comfortable words to his people, told them to make the best of it: "Build houses and live in them; plant gardens and eat what they produce. Take wives and have sons and daughters; take wives for your sons, and give your daughters in marriage. . . . Seek the welfare of the city where I have sent you into exile, and pray to the Lord on its behalf, for in its welfare, you will find your welfare. . . . For surely I know the plans I have for you, says the Lord, plans for your welfare and not for harm, to give you a future with hope." (Jeremiah 29:5–6a, 7, 11.)

Maybe that's what we have to give this woman, hard as her life may be right now: a future with hope. Maybe already her kids are playing road hockey or watching Barney or collecting *Star Wars* action figures. I hope so; I hope she and they will bloom in our colder soil, while bringing to our culture some of the richness of their own. I hope she has found some of her own countrywomen, and maybe together they can have a safe place to put one foot while the other ventures into this strange new world, so safe and bright and prosperous, but so little like home.

Maybe that's how we have to live our lives, even as we long

for the Kingdom: to put down roots and grow where we are, taking pleasure in whatever good the day brings, blessing the world we live in while knowing it isn't the world we want. Maybe if we can do that we really can seek its welfare without trying to force it to be what it cannot be—like learning to love the Canadian winter instead of trying to make it warm. Maybe that way we can give this world our gifts lovingly, instead of trying to shove them down its throat, helping it to change by example instead of trying to pound it into shape by brute force, to our own inevitable defeat.

Maybe that way we can live our lives peaceably and with a measure of contentment, without forgetting what home looks and feels like. Exiles, perhaps, but living in trust that Home will be there when our seventy years are accomplished: living both to love this day and to hope for the future.

The Ants Go
Marching

S ounds of savage banging from the kitchen, where Senior Son
is ant-slaying with the heel of his brother's sneaker. The kid
doesn't have anything against most bugs, but he has a Thing about
ants, which he hates with a fervent, pure, determined passion. As
we are undergoing the annual springtime ant infestation (the first
of many such entomological events, culminating in the annual June
bug window-screen-thwacking marathon), the kid is being kept
busy.

Of course we've anthropomorphized ants as prudent and hard-
working, devoted to the family (hive), modest, forethoughtful.
Which is just plain silly. They are as they are because they have
evolved in particular directions that our ancestors didn't take (or
left behind). But I'm not sure we can talk about one ant realistically, any more than I can talk about one of my liver cells as a freestanding organism. The colony is the true, whole organism; the ant
is a cell of the colony. Maybe what jars my kid is that no individual ant is really an *individual*—more like an elaborated sentient cell

on legs. As one *exceedingly* individual individual, with no use for the conventions, the kid disapproves on instinct of blind conformity.

Ants aren't supposed to have individual personalities—for starters, the hive economy simply wouldn't work if they did. But we are. Aforementioned Senior Son was born with a definite, quite distinct, and highly flavored personality—none of this bland vanilla stuff! His brother was born with a very different but still quite distinct sort of soul flavor. Each of us has our own particular me-ness—like an individual color or personal scent. Unless we are identical twins, we are endowed (usually a blessing, sometimes a bane) with our own personal cell identifiers, genetically programmed, which tell the immune system what is Griselda or Fred and what is non-Griselda or not-Fred. Each of us is a tune unlike any other tune in the whole world, distinct and irreplaceable.

We're born individual. And from there, tragically, we often slide straight downhill. I think probably for some people, life becomes so crushing—starting with bad parenting—that the selfhood gets squished or warped or maybe cut down to a fraction of what God intended. Or maybe it wasn't given nourishment and so failed to thrive and be strong. With decent luck, however, most of us do better. We get pruned here, forced into growth there, sometimes gently, sometimes strongly. We die some necessary small deaths and undergo tiny resurrections (or sometimes even some medium-sized ones). And these forces and events shape us.

Life (God?) has a remarkable facility for teasing out whatever individuality we have, which is probably why institutions for the very elderly are so very full of Extremely Strong Characters, happy or miserable. Somewhere in midlife, most of us turn a corner and start becoming more who we are; the veneer starts coming off and the underlying wood shows through—spruce or mahogany, rough or well polished.

When we hear something like "and he shall purify the sons of Levi," I think most of us get the image of whiter-and-brighter, stainless, well-scrubbed ranks of identical son-of-Levi units. But purifying a metal makes it more *itself*; pure gold is gold-ier than impure gold, and it is not in the least like pure nickel or cadmium. That, I gather, is what Paul means by "perfection": not a bland featurelessness, but a new fullness of being.

Which (of course) doesn't mean that we have the right to impose our egotism over the landscape, indulging our selfishness and making life miserable for others. Purifying metals also requires the burning off of impurities, the separation of pure gold from the slag. But the soul-making process does mean trying to figure out who we are, and what God's apt to want us to become.

And somehow I don't think God wants us to become antlike. I think God likes variety. It's a strange thought: if there really is that Life to Come that many of us believe in, maybe our work when we get there is more of this soul-making process. Maybe all those legions of cherubim and seraphim, instead of being celestial faceless bureaucrats, legions of heavenly ants, are powerfully different individuals, a rainbow of richly individuated personalities, a symphony of wonderfully individual tunes. Now there's a thought to make heaven really *interesting*.

Of one thing I am absolutely sure, from the soles of my feet upward: God knows intimately and lovingly the flavor of every soul who has walked, or is walking, or will ever walk the face of this earth, as well as those who can only sit or lie; and God treasures the differences—the you-ness of you, the me-ness of me.

What we make of this gift of self—whether we train it God-ward or take it in less fruitful directions—is our choice. I suspect our choices sometimes make God weep, and God's sorrow is the deeper because God knows that often our bad choices result from the evil that has been done to us.

But God *knows* us, every smallest strand of who we are, and loves us with a stunning extravagance of love. God's grace is wider and higher and deeper than the firmament of heaven, richer than the Milky Way, more alive than quintillions of ants. God's great desire is for us to be all we can be, most truly and beautifully our own sweet, highly individual souls—and for us to take that bounty of love and wrap ourselves in it, rejoicing.

Maybe not what we except, or deserve, or even really want. But who said grace was in proportion to *anything?*

The Skin of the Earth

On my way home, coming over a bump of the land and seeing laid out before me the neat fields and not so tidy scrub woods, a notion struck me suddenly. The wild trees in these parts are not large or tall—probably no more than forty to fifty feet, most of them; and their roots can't go terribly deep, because there is rock not so far below the surface. So from top to bottom of a tree hereabouts is probably in the neighborhood of eighty feet. Big domestic trees, like my three big storm-scarred maples, are taller and more deeply rooted—maybe as much as a hundred and fifty feet from crown to root bottom. And of course there are places on this earth where the trees get REALLY big; sequoias, I gather, can get up to three hundred and fifty feet, which means with root systems they're probably at least five hundred feet from crown to toes. On the other hand, there are other places, like the High Arctic, where the top-to-bottom of the native flora is maybe a couple of feet, maximum.

Birds, of course, can go higher up than trees, although I don't know how high—maybe a few hundred feet above the land? It can't be too far, because the air becomes too thin to bear them up; and also, why should they go higher than they need to? And of course there are squishy and fascinating things on the sea bed at depths of maybe a couple of thousand feet.

So the life of the earth, from topmost hawk to bottommost sea cucumber, takes place in an up-down range of maybe a mile and a half, unless you count our habit of getting above cloud level in self-propelled tin boxes. Of that life, the vast bulk, both in biomass and number of species, exists within the vertical equivalent of one long city block, just above and just below the face of the planet. Wow.

I don't think it ever occurred to me before, how *thin* this living skin of the earth is. Think of the bulk of the planet, and think of the thickness of the biosphere, and you realize that the area where we live and breathe and go about our daily business and make love and bear babies and die and hurt and rejoice and all that is *far* thinner than a thin layer of paint on a very big beach ball. Now there is a thought to sit down in front of and stare at for a while. That's something to make you go outside and find a piece of lawn, or a patch of woods, or a city park, and simply *look* at it in bemusement and wonder.

And yet, thin doesn't mean fragile. This skin may be thin, but it's as tough as spider's silk (which has a tensile strength greater than the very best steel). It is tremendously tenacious. However we wound it, tearing at it in our selfishness, life pushes its way back, healing itself, regulating itself. If (as seems increasingly likely these days) we eventually do ourselves in through climate change, turning most of this earth into desert and swamp and wasting ourselves out of existence, this skin-of-the-earth thing will wait us out, go through another of its transitions, and come back in a new form, with or without us.

What fascinates me, though, is not just the thinness and toughness of this skin, but its connectedness. The grass in your backyard uptakes the carbon dioxide from my compost bin and produces oxygen for the dog next door, whom my cats torment. The cat long ago buried in the old vegetable garden (we put his body down a groundhog hole) has long since been converted into carbon dioxide and is probably part of the spruce trees by now. You simply cannot take one bit of this skin in isolation, not without making the conditions hopelessly artificial. It is a unity, and we are part of it.

We are part of a unity with each other, too; your suffering should make me weep, and my joy should make you laugh. One of the worst things we do to ourselves and each other is to erect divisions where none should exist. I guess we feel overwhelmed otherwise, and maybe for that reason it's necessary. If you could truly feel all the pain out there, it would swamp you—imagine what we put God through, that way! But the fact remains that when we look at each other or ourselves as freestanding noninterdependent units, we're lying in Mother Nature's face. Because there is no such thing alive on the face of this earth.

Look at it, this thin, tough skin, in all its beauty and complexity, and think, this is what God made: "The earth is the Lord's and all that is in it; the world and those who live in it; for he has founded it on the seas, and established it on the rivers." Take this creation seriously, for this is the work God knows and loves infinitely better than we ever can: "Who laid its cornerstone when the morning stars sang together and all the heavenly begins shouted for joy?"

It is God's green earth, and it nourishes and sustains us. Take time to wonder at its complexity—at God's "inordinate fondness for beetles," at the shape of an elm, at the miraculous properties of water, at the beauty of a squirrel scrambling through the branches, the shape of the pigeon's breast. Pay attention to it. Turn it over in your mind. Go look at it, and think of that thin, tough, exuberant, resilient skin of life, and smile.

Think of God's joy in this creation. And do it no harm.

Under Construction

They're hard at work on the main interchange for our town—the one between our east-west highway and the new four-lane highway into the city. Earth-moving machines bumble like humongous bugs, hauling soil from point A to point B, building up the ramps and overpass. The site is crawling with guys putting up forms and pouring concrete. It's a four-year-old boy's idea of heaven on earth.

I was out too, leading into town for less large and grandiose purposes—picking up some stuff from the office and meeting a friend for lunch—and found myself stopped, waiting for some big-bug earth movers to bounce across from one earth mound to another. It took a while. While I waited for the bored signal-woman's sign to flip from STOP to SLOW, I watched a power shovel gently scratch up a ton or so of soil, dump it about fif-teen feet from its source, and then smooth and pat it flat with surprisingly delicate back-and-forth motions of its huge toothed bucket. I know this is antropomorphizing (felinopomorphizing?)

but the shovel looked almost playful, like a vastly overgrown kitten playing boogeties.

I have no idea *why* that scoopful of soil needed to go from Point A to Point B; you couldn't tell a thing from the general mess. That small patch of beaten-up landscape didn't look like part of a ditch or ramp or overpass. But the operator was most likely tossing this bucket of schloop around for a reason. Presumably the results will become clearer in time.

We would all, of course, love to have God skywriting for us: "You are going through this particular whatever-it-is right now because in six months' time you are going to be over *here* and I have to nudge you around a bit first to get you correctly lined up and ready." To quote that most estimable figure, Daffy Duck, "Ha. It is to laugh." Life doesn't work that way. Only long after the fact can we look back and figure out what the pattern was. At the time, we seemed to be stumbling in confusion through what we later see to have a dance of some complexity.

Maybe we won't find out for years what the pattern was. Maybe for some of the greater patches of obscurity in life we won't figure it out at all in this life—maybe that discovery waits on the other side of the River. But often it feels as though God leaves us here in the mud and muddle, trying desperately to be patient and trustful and usually not managing either very well.

It's particularly hard because, when you're in the middle of what seems like a hellacious big mess, you cannot possibly sort out what's God's purpose and what's not—what's God's will or what's the result of your own sometimes misguided will, or the misguided wills of others whose influence over your life may be profound and anything but beneficial. A friend came back from a month in Bangladesh and says quite firmly that she couldn't see God anywhere there, not one bit, theology be damned, and sometimes life is indeed like that: simply too chaotic to see God anywhere at all.

I wish I could say, "Always do this thing or that thing, and it will all be okay," but I've rarely found a simple rule that couldn't easily be misused. Sometimes it's right to embrace, sometimes it's best to refrain from embracing. Sometimes it's right to forgive; sometimes it's right to say, "No, that was wrong and I will not accept it from you." Sometimes it's right to laugh or weep or roar with anger; sometimes it's best to bide in disciplined quiet. But if we think a particular choice is simple black and white, it's almost always either because the decision doesn't matter much, or because we haven't given it nearly enough thought.

It helps to keep the end in mind. We don't carry out of life our actions and achievements; we leave them behind, and they will be as dust in a thousand years or so, as this new intersection will be— probably a whole lot sooner than that for the vast majority of us. We may be scrupulously orthodox and rigidly lawful, righteous in our anger against what is Clearly Wrong, doing nothing in contravention to Scripture and Tradition, and still be as shriveled and sour as pickled gherkins. We may fall off the wagon and tumble into stupidities and be clowns and lost sheep and prodigal children and still fetch up as golden, generous hearts, full of joy and compassion, making God smile. That's what's at the end of this sometimes bewildering process: taking our souls, whatever we and God and life have made of them, to show the God who made us.

The one thing I am sure of is this: if you live life trusting in God's love and power and good purposes, and if you do your best to conform to the Great Commandment, putting it above all other laws and prophets—then whatever God and you and life make of your life, God and life and you will make something good for you. Make your choices accordingly.

Invite the Spirit to direct your ways, welcoming it into your life, and have faith in God's love and in the path Christ blazed for us through the wilderness. Live with a view of the Kingdom in the corner of your eye, remembering always that it is a place of deep delight, and however muddled your life may seem now, in the end it will indeed all come round right.

Road in the Wilderness

The paving train is out in ponderous, inexorable force, laying down what is (I suspect) the last layer of asphalt on the next stretch of four-lane highway connecting my town to the city. Pretty soon it should be four-lane all the way out to the road by the river. South of that, the road cut is still raw and wounded-looking. The big interchange for the main east-west highway still swarms with hard-hatted guys laying forms and setting steel rods before the concrete is poured. That stretch still has a long way to go.

What popped into my head, as I drove north past the paving train, toward the city for an appointment, was the line from Isaiah: "Make straight in the desert a highway for your God." I'd heard the line sung a gazillion times in *Messiah*, but I'd never really given it any real thought before. What does it *mean*, anyway? So I spent the rest of the trip time thinking about highways, what they are, what they mean, how we make them.

It's a given, in Christian belief, that God profoundly respects our freedom—that God does not come where God is not invited.

Fair enough; that's one possible obvious meaning for the line. We're supposed to take steps to open up the way for God, because God insists on respecting our boundaries. That's the quick, pat theological answer.

But such a simple answer begs the metaphor. There's too much in that image for a quick, pat answer, theologically correct or not. It feels like there are underlayers of meaning, pleading to be unpacked.

Desert. Why would God need a highway through the desert? Presumably God knows where God is going, after all, and presumably God can get through the desert quite unaided by human intervention. It's not like getting through the Ontario cedar swamps, after all; there are no trees in the way, although I suppose loose sand could be a real bogging-down problem.

Back off the word "desert" for a moment. Desert would have been the background landscape for the people Isaiah was preaching for—what lay outside the boundaries of town and farmland. The equivalent here is brush woods—it used to be tall stands of virgin pine, but they were wiped out a century ago. But maybe our landscape will do as well for Isaiah's words: can we say "make straight through the bush a highway for our God"? Yes. Sounds right, feels right.

But still, it doesn't make literal sense. The Spirit can get from here to Moosonee without my intervention. The Spirit can get all the way to Tuktoyaktuk, for that matter, to Iqaluit and Frobisher Bay. The Spirit can wander over the great gray beautiful Canadian Shield, through the real bush—a thousand miles of it, peaceful and immense and of formidable quietness—over hundreds of miles of tundra, with its low and quiet beauty. The Spirit blows where the Spirit damn well pleases, after all.

But can the Spirit get to the middle of *me* without my cooperation? What about my own waste and desert spaces, my own tangles of cedar, my own personal internal swamps and sloughs? Can this Spirit travel into my inmost places, where the deep fears and hurts are, where there lurk black bears of anger and burned-out timberlands of ancient grief? "Can" is irrelevant. Won't. Not without my permission. My job is to open the road, not for God's sweet sake, but for my own. It's that act of will that God waits for.

Maybe—I don't know!—God could get through my wilderness just for the asking. But maybe God's work in me goes faster and better if I actively help—if I dig out the rocks, clear out the scrub timber, fill in the swamps and sinkholes, build up a roadbed, making it as straight and level as my inner landscape allows. This is a two-way business, after all, a dance, not a solo performance by either God or me.

Maybe there are other reasons as well. Our purpose in this life is to glorify God and love each other. When we make roads into our own wildernesses, we build paths for each other to travel, in that exchange of love that is what God intended us to live in. Maybe we need paths for ourselves to travel, for that matter, exploring what lies in our own interior landscape—for which of us truly knows his or her own heart?

Whatever the reason, I have to head out into that wilderness, that country beyond the town and farmlands, where I'm alone with my self and the Spirit, and once there, I must get working, exploring and clearing and building, preparing a highway for my

God. I hope the mosquitoes aren't too fierce and the black bears behave themselves. I hope that there is cool spring water in the heat of the day, and that the Spirit's singing will keep me from getting too lonely. But I'm called to this labor, as are we all.

And in the end we will shout for joy, and be tenderly carried like beloved lamb-children, and be comforted at the close of the day, when the work is finished and we rest in that Light that we can now not begin to imagine.

Critters

Quite swiftly now, the new four-lane highway is sweeping its way out in our direction. By the end of the summer it will connect us to the city easily, swiftly, and far more safely than the old infamous two-lane killer highway that I know like the back of my hand. And as the big road comes our way, so too do many more people. We're getting built up out here, as people look for space and tranquility and the natural peaceful life. On the whole, they're very welcome. But unfortunately, some of them have forgotten one fundamental fact:

It is a truth universally acknowledged, that the countryside is full of critters.

Take for example the city lady out hiking with our group a few weeks ago, before the biting insects were properly out, who sidled up to the hike leader and asked if he couldn't do something to get rid of "these bugs"—these bugs being perfectly innocent bitty gnats that weren't even swarming much. Was he supposed to spray the entire forest with Raid? Or take the woman who built herself a fine new rock garden at her fine new country house—and then called up our local wildlife officer in hysterics because snakes were sunning themselves all over her artfully arranged boulders. Then there's the cursing up and down new country lanes as it begins to dawn on ex-urbanites that you do NOT put out bagged garbage the night before it's to be collected, because Wild Things look at the bags and murmur, "Lunch!"

It's funny how many of our problems result from our entirely unrealistic expectations of what Life is Supposed to be Like. I don't see inscribed anywhere on my birth certificate a promise that life was going to be easy or simple—and yet a part of me deeply resents the fact that it isn't easy or simple, as though I had a right to that. When we yell, "Why me?" it doesn't occur to us to ask ourselves why it *shouldn't* be me. Why *not* me? Why anyone at all? Who made me exempt?

Another feature of rural life: the periodic pumping out of the septic tank. The last time the good sewage-pumping people came around with their big truck and their hose and pump and set to work to drain our system, I couldn't resist the temptation: I asked one of the guys, "So what got you into this business?" He must get asked this question a dozen times a week, because he popped back without a second thought, "Shit happens."

It does. Gnats happen. Snakes happen. June bugs happen, noisily and clumsily. Flying ants happen. Pain happens. Injustice happens. Evil happens, though fortunately so does Good. The psalmist noted, back a couple-three thousand years ago, that rain falls on the wicked and the just alike. This is not exactly news. So why do we find it so outrageous and insupportable?

Spring

We expect to be punished for being Bad and rewarded for being Good, because that's what we've been told as children; and yet it often doesn't work that way. Free will (ours or others') and natural processes—these are the jokers, the wild cards, that may enroll us in the Trauma Club even when we've been good as gold.

We can howl into the wind over the injustice of it all, and obsess about our wrongs and injuries and ill-fortune. We may let our hurt and rage pickle our souls until we're sour and hardened and shriveled with resentment, like a cucumber kept too long in brine. Or, with the Spirit nudging us in better directions, we can take whatever life has handed us and see what good we can make of it. Or—even better—we can see what good it can make of us.

I've been out in this little rural town a few years now, and I never put my garbage out until the morning of garbage day, and I weather the annual invasion of flying ants and coexist with the spiders and mosquitoes. I'm actually fond of the June bugs for their sheer endearing stupidity. My garage often has nondomestic mammals going squeak and rustle in it. We coexist; we share a property, and nobody gets her or its knickers in a twist about it.

But I promise to let God and Nature make of me whatever the two of them will have me become, because I have learned that it's better that way than for me to try to make of God and Nature what I want them to be. They're bigger than I am, God and Nature; they're older, and stronger, and I trust their judgment. We don't argue. It's better that way.

Part Six

Summer

For the Birds

I don't know whether there were far more birds than normal or whether I simply was in a bird-noticing mood as I walked out to the store by the path past the pine grove. I'm not a birder, but I like birds. They make life a little richer, a little happier. We share a world amicably enough, but in general I probably pay them about as much attention as they pay me, which is not much.

But for some reason, that morning, my walk seemed remarkably be-birded. I don't know a thing about bird names, but a whole bunch of sociable little guys (sparrows, maybe?) seemed almost to be flirting with me. They'd light in the road chirping, take off as soon as I got within a certain distance, swirl up and circle around, fly a little way, alight, chirp, dart off, settle down. . . . It felt more like a game than anything else.

An obviously paired pair (mourning doves, maybe? mates or competitors or just friends?) were whooping it up through the pine grove, easily dodging the trees as they chased each other. Blue jays I can definitely recognize, and I saw one, a flash of bright boldness, as well as one definite goldfinch (impossible to miss!). I saw a solemn heron flying, its legs trailing out behind it and its big wings slowly beating the air. But I cannot for the life of me tell you the name of the handsome gray jobbie with the black-and-white trim who was picking bugs out of a pine tree's bark. I'm sure a birder would know, but I didn't have a clue.

It would be anthropomorphizing to say that the birds were happy. I thought as I watched them how unutterably foreign their experience is to mine—how little I could possibly ever understand how it feels to be a bird. Birds don't, in fact, go where they will; they have boundaries both territorial and behavioral; they are constricted by instinct. I suppose in one sense we're freer than they are—or at least those of us who live in freedom are.

Birds may respect their own boundaries, but they have no use for the lines we draw on the earth or for the walls we build. They have their own imperatives instead. (Some years ago a peregrine falcon built its nest on a ledge of an Ottawa skyscraper and used to startle the bureaucrats and gray-breasted businesspersons by dive-bombing the sidewalk for pigeons, a fact I found obscurely cheering.) And because we can't fly, birds represent something to humans: a lightness of being, freedom, play, and also perhaps courage and boldness. Maybe that's why we use the symbol of a dove for the Holy Spirit, to try to picture that freedom: "The wind blows where it will and cannot be stopped."

I thought, watching the cloud of little guys lift and swirl away, how joyous they made me feel, and I remembered a line from W. H. Auden—I don't know where I read it. He said, "One's duty to God is to be happy." It's not always a duty we can carry out. I thought of a recent tragedy—a young man killed in a freak accident on a fairway ride in Ottawa. It would be insulting his parents to suggest that they have a duty to God to be happy. Their job, right now, is to mourn for a necessary season, and to skimp that process would be wrong. Telling people to be joyful under supremely unjoyful conditions, like grief or real oppression or physical pain or illness, may be really saying only, "Live with it. I don't want to deal with your problems. I don't want to suffer with you. You're making me uncomfortable, and I don't want to be uncomfortable." Reality-denial is neither sweet nor wholesome. And telling people in "sorrow, trouble, need, sickness" to rejoice can, instead of comforting them, be deeply maddening to anyone whose brain has not been turned off at source. Maybe there's Joy to be found even in those circumstances, but that's for the sufferer to discover for him- or herself—as Job did when the Lord told him to get his nose out of his navel and look around at Creation—not for others to get all condescending about.

But when joy *is* reasonably possible, or even maybe a little bit before that, I think it is indeed what we owe God—not so much to *feel* joy as to experience Joy. "Oh, be joyful in the Lord, all ye lands," as the psalmist said: a reasonable instruction. If that doesn't seem possible, it may be because we're confusing Joy and happiness, which are very different things. Happiness, or satisfaction or pleasure, are our own internal reactions. But Joy isn't ours; it's God's, and God is trying to get us to notice it. Joy lies outside ourselves, waiting for us to tumble into it, trip and sit down in it with a splash, learning to laugh at ourselves in the process..

Joy lurks—in a bunch of small birds, in the shadows of a green bush, in the turn of a child's wrist or the curve of a man's shoulder, in almost any given flower. It can hit you like a ton of bricks when you're just standing there at the kitchen counter getting supper. It may waylay you on the highway or seduce you while you're talking to a friend or jump you in the supermarket for no reason at all. You just have to allow that it may be possible, and let it make you happy.

We can ignore Joy, because we're so wrapped up in our own self-chosen miseries, cherishing this grievance or that grief and therefore resolutely refusing to accept Joy's existence. Or we may fall in love with the Byronic Rrrrromantic Misery of Things—the misery part usually stemming from the fact that others have, most unfairly, failed to worship my ego as my ego would like to be worshiped. Life disappoints us deeply by failing to conserve our childhood certainty that we are at the center of the known universe.

But if we lift up our eyes and look around, Joy's out there, wanting to be found. It wants to infect us, if we're willing to lay ourselves open to it, even a little.

It's waiting out there with the birds. Go look for it.

Willpower

(FOR ALBERTA EVA GATES GREENOUGH, 1905-97)

When I met her, twenty-some years, ago, she was a mere sprig of barely seventy, retired after almost fifty years of elementary school teaching, but still full of beans. She ran her household as she always had, baking her own bread, watching her bank accounts, keeping her mildly cheerless overdecorated house in apple-pie order. Each summer she moved upcountry and put in her garden and canned her preserves. The culture she'd been born and bred in had been essentially a nineteenth-century one, and she still had those values: industry, thriftiness, "a good tub stands on its own bottom," a strong sense of conventional morality, order, regularity. But she had a mildly wicked streak as well, which I liked.

What I didn't like so well was her will, which was extremely formidable. I had to admire it, the way you might admire, say, a well-built tank on maneuvers, or perhaps a bull elephant or a *really* big diesel engine. It was a sort of force of nature all by itself. To fulfill it, to get what it dictated, she would use any tactics from tears to nagging to full-fledged hysteria. But I had the oddest sense that her will was almost independent of her, if that makes any sense—of her, but also oddly separate from her, like a symbiotic organism.

I could see how it had gotten so large and strong, this Percheron of a will. She had survived tragedy and a truly horrible childhood, had pulled herself up to become a teacher (and a good one) with a proper professionalism and an excellent reputation. Her willpower had got her her man and her child and her respectable little house in the city and the country cottage with its vegetable garden. Of course there were costs: her man died young, for his family, and her child wasn't as obedient as she wanted. But on the whole her will had been a good servant to her.

It was her will that her child take the city house, so that happened (against the child's will!) and she settled into the country place. And then, as the years passed, something began to happen that was every bit against her will, but she couldn't stop it. She aged. A little at a time, she gave up this and that, as she could no longer manage. She said, half petulant, half (apparently) insouciant, "Oh, I can't be *bothered*"—pretending half to herself, half to the rest of us, that this giving up was of her own choosing. She stopped driving. She gave up the vegetable garden. She abandoned bridge games and church. She started to eat poorly, and her house grew dirty and wildly overstuffed as her thriftiness grew more compulsive. Life contracted around her, but she stubbornly clung to her dearest possession: her independence, her freedom to live as she wanted—the ability to give her will full rein.

For as she aged and grew weaker as a person, her will grew stronger. It had been her servant all her life, but now it seemed to be taking on a life of its own. I wonder if it became her master. I'm not sure who was on the chain and who was leading it, for a while there. And her will was extremely unattractive: a noisy and demanding brat, full of rage because the rest of the world wouldn't drop everything to do its bidding. Her will started to drive people away from her; they got tired of being told to drop everything and do what she wanted RIGHT NOW. But she needed people to survive, because she could no longer manage by herself. Her will, dominating her and everyone around her, had driven her into an impossible position. She was trapped, slowly sliding into lonely paranoia and physical illness and filth, because her will wouldn't let her consider any compromise that could have allowed her to keep at least part of her independence. It would not bend so far.

The crisis came when she was eighty-six and could no longer manage on her own. Her family found a good retirement house and moved her into it, kicking and screaming. The struggle was titanic, but in the end she lost. For a full five years her will fought the change tooth and nail, with all her formidable strength. This was not what she wanted, and she said so, at length, for years. She made herself wretched; she made everyone within earshot miserable; she made the staff's life hellish; she terrorized the proprietors of the retirement home. She rebelled with every fiber of her being. Her aging body had betrayed her will, but her will was as strong as ever, all the cover stripped away from it, bright and clear as pure polished steel. It knew what it wanted. It always had, after all.

Last year she broke her hip, and that put her in a wheelchair; she had to move into a nursing home. I haven't seen her, so I don't know how she took the change. Not well, I gather. She'd been saying for years that someone should take her out behind the barn and shoot her. A couple of weeks ago, she began to slide—nothing obvious, just extreme old age. Last Sunday, she simply stopped breathing. She was ninety-one.

I'd thought badly of her in some ways—too harshly, I think now, looking back. The funny thing is, looking back: she really was in many ways a good person, and certainly she tried hard. So I don't really have any serious doubts that the Lord will have called her to Him, welcoming her.

I have this vision of God holding out His hand as her soul reaches Him, bidding her to put her will in it, as a gift to Him. I'm not sure she could have done that a few years ago; I think she might have turned her back on God rather than bend her will one fraction. But maybe something softened and broke within her in the last little while; I don't know. She went gently, without a struggle, so I'm hopeful. If she's made her gift of Will to God—and it mustn't be a purchase of anything or a bribe, but a free gift of her own volition—then she is now in so much joy in that land beyond the River.

As C. S. Lewis wrote, "There are only two kinds of people in the end: those who say to God, 'Thy will be done,' and those to whom God says, in the end, '*Thy* will be done.' All that are in Hell choose it. Without that self-choice there could be no Hell."* I don't know why, but I have the sense that in the end she chose Heaven, handing over her will like a child handing over a toy it had loved

*C. S. Lewis, *The Great Divorce* (London: Fount, 1977), pp. 66–67.

but lost interest in. If she made that surrender, God would give her will back to her, cleaned of all its egotism and selfishness, strong and ardent as ever, but newly aligned in the deep, happy harmony she never found in this life.

May her soul, freed of the heavy self-burden of will it bore for so many years, now rest quiet and happy, cupped in the palm of God's loving hand, at peace and in joy.

Shades

These days I wear clip-on sunglasses when I drive into the city. I've become photosensitive; very bright daylight makes me feel sick and shaky. The shades help; so does a large straw hat. Was driving into the office yesterday, all protectively be-shaded, when I realized to my discomfiture that something was mildly wrong. Things looked . . . not quite right. It took me awhile, but I finally figured out what the problem was.

Now this has been an incredible year for flowers, domestic and wild: I have never seen such hollyhocks, such pansies and petunias, such an uproar of coreopsis, of daisies and black-eyed Susans and you-have-it. Even *my* poor garden has a few flowers, which should tell you. Purple loosestrife, noxious but gorgeous, is running riot right now, along with masses of Queen Anne's lace and something yellow I don't know the name of.

And it all looked wrong with sunglasses on.

It's not like the gentle dulling of cloudy light or rain; that sort of quiet, true light merely intensifies the natural colors. The colors become more themselves in softer light. No, this was different: filtering the light shifted the colors into shades that were slightly off and far less interesting. Take the purple loosestrife (please!). It normally flowers in quite a cheerful shade of fuchsia—its one redeeming characteristic, since otherwise it's a real predatory summovabitch of a plant. Seen with sunglasses on, it went through a tint shift that made it dull, flattened, almost boring, without becoming one whit less obnoxiously aggressive. I didn't like that.

In fact, once I started thinking about it, I made a discovery: I may need the sunglasses, but I don't like them, and not just because they make Mother Nature look like she needs a good laxative. They didn't improve the cityscape either.

I don't like the way sunglasses make the face that's wearing them inaccessible. If a person's soul looks out of the person's eyes, then what do sunglasses do? If I'm wearing them and you aren't, then my face is guarded, invulnerable, private—in fact, that's why some people wear shades—while yours is still naked to my hidden eye. Your only real defense is to guard your own face, either with shades of your own or with that woodenly expressionless blankness that poses for Being Cool, until a person realizes how silly it really is. And if you guard your face, I have to guard mine more closely, and so on and so forth, until we both might as well wear something carved in elm on the front of our noggins. Not a positive way of operating, I think. Whatever closes us off from danger also closes us off from opportunity. Whatever shuts the door on human contact also shuts the door on love.

Sunglasses are about filtering—about accepting only the amount of light we feel we can comfortably handle, and only the wavelengths we like. We find ways of hiding from what we don't like, whether it's strong sunlight, being looked at, our own shortcomings, or the pain of the world.

Filters may be necessary, but that doesn't make them a good thing. When I flip past the magazine photo spread on the horrors going on in the Sudan, without really looking at it—in fact, quite purposefully skipping the story—I am filtering. If I had to take that reality into myself properly—that hollow-cheeked baby fruitlessly sucking its mother's collapsed and shriveled breast—it would hurt so horribly. So I filter it out. I have enough on my plate already, I think; I can't do anything about this suffering anyway. No use getting my knickers into a twist about it.

Very true. And from there it's a very short step to ignoring the beggar on the street, or filtering out the victims of abuse. ("Why don't you just get *over* it instead of bothering the rest of us?") It becomes possible to see any sharp brightness or strong shadow as being obtrusive and painful, until we find ourselves wanting to live in a dim world, free of corners or discomfort. But that's not what God expects of us, because that's no way to grow a soul. God takes on the pain of the Sudan, takes it into Godself and redeems it, and that means I should be able to look at that reality with compassion, but without flinching. Because that's how we grow our souls—not by filtering out the things we think we can't handle, but by learning slowly to handle them, a little at a time. Sometimes we may genuinely need filters. But we should always be aware that they have their price: less pain, maybe, but also less joy.

In this life, I'm probably always going to need some protection from full sunlight, but in the next I will accommodate to brightness. In this world I may need to see through these glasses, darkly, but in the next I will learn to accept and welcome and increasingly rejoice in the Light. Unfiltered.

Jesse

(FOR JESSE'S AUNT JAN, WITH FOND MEMORIES OF
THREE-IN-ONE OIL ON A TRINITY SUNDAY MORNING)

We're going to miss Jesse. He was a summer intern in our office, a bright, lively, likable kid of nineteen, a real asset to our firm. Yesterday was his last full day; he's off to his second year in university next week. He should do well there, if he can ever get into the habit of finishing projects. I like talking with Jesse, who is a sociable guy and a lot of fun. It came up quite in passing that I'm an Anglican; his aunt, whom I know slightly, is an Anglican priest. Jesse and the rest of his family are cheerful atheists, tending (when they think of it at all) toward a mild interest in Zen and some undefined Spirit of the Universe. It's funny; I know I'm supposed to feel as though I ought to proselytize people like Jesse, but I just don't feel the need.

On a corner down the street from our office, a street evangelist was going at it last week, bellowing at (and largely past) the crowds at lunchtime—a tall, strongly built, middle-aged man, neatly dressed, standing rigid as a board and making punching motions to emphasize his message. One or two people were listening. Most of those within earshot were trying to pretend that either he or they were somewhere else. On a whim, I walked up and stood in front of him, wanting to see his reaction. I touched the cross I wore at my throat, a plain thing given to me in Love by a List brother. The street preacher looked right past me as though I weren't there, and began to holler about people who wear Jesus as fine jewelry around their necks but hate him in their hearts. Maybe I'm wrong or imagining things, but it felt as though a huge hostility, born of fear, was coming from him in waves, like the smell of nicotine from a smoker's clothing. I said to him, "This is counter-evangelism," and he went on roaring, "You must be born AGAIN, you miserable sinners!"

It does no good to rant at people like Jesse about the need to be "born again." And we aren't all born again overnight; some of us are brought to birth so slowly, so gently, we might as well say (as one man did), "I was born again starting sometime around 1979, but I don't think I'm done yet." So far as I can tell, I don't think Jesse feels any particular need of Christianity at this stage in his life. He may very well feel that need in God's good time (not mine!). But that's really between Jesse and God. If and as the time comes for him to find God, I think I can trust God to make the right moves, most likely through other people in Jesse's life. Obviously others aren't in the same position as Jesse and may be in real need of more active intervention—especially those who feel broken or are near a breaking point. But at this point I'm inclined to look at Jesse and think, "If it ain't broke yet, don't try to fix it." The kid obviously has excellent ethical sense and a good nose for falseness or pretension. Whether or not he accepts the Word from the neck up, he behaves more like a Christian than not.

Some babies need to be wrapped tightly, to feel safe and snug and secure, and are not happy unless they're closely swaddled. Others, more venturesome, need to kick; wrap them tight and they'll roar in frustration. People like Jesse don't feel a need for the safe snugness of orthodoxy. His is a wriggly, happy, confident, damn-the-torpedoes soul. He wants to play with God, perhaps. And God could enjoy playing with Jesse, I suspect.

But what the Jesses of this world may feel in time is that there's something missing, something incomplete in their otherwise fine and cheerful lives. Some of us reach for God when life has forced us to a breaking point. Others feel a sort of hollowness, a gentle ache, as though something impalpable is missing. Jesse spoke of his stepfather's workaholism, and that's something that some people use to fill the aching hole; others turn to materialism or drink or golf or other people or therapy or model railroading. But as Salman Rushdie said, it's a God-shaped hole.

If the safety of orthodoxy isn't apt to fetch Jesse to God, something else might, in the long run: and that's the sense that some Christians manage to exude: not love, but Love. At its best and clearest, it comes across as a sort of quiet happiness, a deep inner peace, a freedom and playfulness, and a sense of inward balance and wholeness. It delights in human souls of all hues and dispositions and particulars, feeling their shadows as sad, without any deep need to judge or fix or condemn. That sort of Christianity might fetch Jesse, because it offers him something that his own world cannot provide.

The beauty of any good religion is that it leaves space for both. Some people really do need that sense of safety, comfort, continu-

ance, that underlies a proper orthodoxy. Nothing wrong with
them. Others, like Jesse, who have praxis in their bones and
boundless self-confidence, need the freedom to quest and imagine
and explore. Of course they need to test their findings against
Scripture and tradition, to make sure they don't wander off in
strange directions. But they don't need to be told spiritual truths;
they need to discover spiritual truths on their own.

Why do we assume that God loves us so little that we must
be perfect conformists, saying all the right words and doing all the
right things, or be judged and condemned? I cannot believe in a
God who would say that the street-corner preacher was Saved and
Jesse is Damned because the preacher is saying the right words and
Jesse is not. God only knows what's in the preacher's soul, but he
certainly wasn't projecting Christian love. Why can't we just trust
God to get on with us and others, giving God permission to use
us as God sees fit? Maybe because it's so much easier to bellow the
Word at others than to take it into our own souls and learn to
teach it properly, through love: "Always preach the gospel. When
necessary, use words."

Grace Waiting

(FOR ROBERT MCAFEE BROWN AND HIS FAMILY)

The stack of stuff in the corner of the dining room has grown steadily over the last couple of weeks. Tent, sleeping bags, air mattresses, camping stove and fuel, lantern, batteries, tarp, blankets ... In a week's time I'll have jammed all this stuff into my small silver car and, with a friend, I will start out for my favorite corner of God's earth: a small high-up piece of northwestern Massachusetts. We plan to camp there and to do a lot of walking in the Berkshires. I'm looking forward to this trip much more than I would even to a proper holiday in beautiful country with the best of good company. This place where we're going—it and I go back a ways.

To when I was nine, in fact, and my parents and sisters and I were staying with good family friends, in their big eighteenth-century clapboard farmhouse at the end of a dirt road. The road petered off into a path through the woods, and the woods were purely magic. I remember standing on the path staring into those woods, which were damp and ferny and deep and very, very green. And at that moment I experienced for the first time that sense of Something—of mystery, of richness, of an infinitely desirable Real lurking over the next ridge, down deep in the next dell. Whatever it was, I knew intuitively I could never lay hands on in, however far I tried to follow it. Even then, I think I knew that some things have to wait for another life, another country. But still, this place always had the smell of whatever-it-was, and I loved the place for that smell, which I still associate with ferny woods, and for its beauty, for it is a very beautiful place.

It was maybe ten years later, when I was more arrogant and substantially more foolish, that I let myself be argued into believing that what I'd experienced was a figment of my imagination. Young adulthood can be an age at which religion and spirituality seem silly and self-indulgent, as does much of what's normally felt and experienced. It's easy to be head-driven and idealistic and harshly ascetic, and therefore to dismiss realities that have no place in syllogisms and cannot be solidly documented. Some people remain mired in that phase and see it as the only real maturity. Others learn better. But when I was young and foolish I allowed myself to be divorced from whatever-it-is that I smelled in those woods, to be convinced that the something-over-the-ridge probably wasn't real; or if it was real, it didn't much matter; or if it mattered, then there was something wrong with me because it shouldn't matter, logically speaking.

Well, it was a long road back from that mistaken choice, and it involved retracing all sorts of wrong turnings and untangling knots in a slow and extremely painful process. I had a lot to unlearn and relearn before, last summer, I could turn again at the store in the village and take the steep, winding road back up between the knees of the hills; turn again at the old graveyard and drive slowly down the dirt road through the ferny woods to the old farmhouse. I'd been away for so very many years. But the smell's still there, and the woods are still deep and green, promising that Real whatever-it-is off in the next dell, behind the next ridge, beyond this life's reach. In short, nothing has changed.

What on earth possesses us to imagine, for even a moment, that we can really live without faith? Maybe if we've never found faith in the first place, it's different—but I'd had that knowledge of the Something from the time I'd looked deep into those woods. I think maybe all healthy children have that knowledge. But where, in my young arrogance and idealism, did I get off believing I could make do without faith? Why did I so deeply mistrust the imprint it had left on my soul? Why was I so ready to listen to the whisper saying, "It's only your imagination; none of this is real"?

Why do we so easily assume that the world of the spirit is ersatz? Mind you, if we see God as being a conjuror popping rabbits out of hats in response to prayer, then we're apt to see faith as fraudulent when the rabbit fails to appear. If we think we can buy God by being Good or following The Rules, we're most likely in for a similar disillusionment. But I don't think that conjuror-God was in my woods, all those years ago; that was not the Being I felt deep in the ferny woods. I think I sensed some music beyond the reach of human hearing. That's as near as I can get to it.

I don't know how we can bear to be parted from faith once we've found it, without doing deep damage to our souls. But I do know that, blessedly, faith is so forgiving that it's simply relieved to be picked up again; it doesn't get angry at you for laying it down, walking away, and forgetting about it. It's just glad to be held again, regardless. Hold out your arms and it leaps into them. We talk about God's judgment and righteousness, but does it ever occur to us to wonder if perhaps God is simply delighted to be *remembered*? Even hatred is easier to bear than indifference, after all.

God doesn't have to punish us for being unfaithful; if we are unfaithful, we'll have all the punishment we need in our self-chosen hells. But when we turn back faithward, there it is outwaiting us, ever patient, always wanting us, always longing to fetch us home. And then we learn, to our incredulity, that we really *are* beloved of God. Wow.

So next weekend I'll turn off at the store at the village and climb up the winding road again, and I have no doubt at all that the ferny damp smell will be there, and the deep light in the woods, and that sense of there being Something just over the ridge, deeper in the next dell, that I can't reach and don't particularly want or need to reach now. I am content with what I can reach in this life, knowing that the Other will be there in God's own good time—in kairos. Some things are best savored later.

Whatever happens, I've learned to have faith in faith itself. It does not go away. It waits with infinite patience until we realize that we want it, and then, when we're willing to admit that we do need and want it, it welcomes us home with such deep and happy quiet, with such loving untroubled joy.

MacGyvering

Our camp's dining room consisted of a picnic table with a propane stove and a dishpan, all roofed over and made dry and roomlike by a blue plastic tarp. Putting up the tarp was half the battle and much of the fun.

Of course I'd known I'd need the tarp, and ropes, and the ties to fix the tarp to the ropes, and a pole or two, just in case. I'd planned for that and brought what I needed—except for the can of corned beef hash, but that came later. There's no point planning how you're going to put up a tarp when you're camping; you don't know what the site's going to be like. So you MacGyver it.

"MacGyver" was a TV show in which the hero improvised his way out of Interesting Situations without violence and with very ordinary things—a Swiss army knife, duct tape, whatever. To MacGyver is, therefore, to wing it with whatever comes to hand.

The first steps in setting up the dining shelter were self-evident: table over here, tarp slung from lines between conveniently placed trees. We tied the tarp to the ropes, guying the corners and propping the center up with a pole set on top of the picnic table. All fine and snug—until, on the second day, it rained as it rains in the mountains, good and heavy. We loosened this line, retied that one, untied the tarp in one spot to make a rain gutter, and finally (the master touch!) propped up the central pole with the upended (clean and empty) can from the previous supper's corned beef hash. That put the roof peak at the perfect angle to drain properly. Worked like a charm. Pure MacGyvering on a small and simple scale, most satisfying.

We would all, of course, like to microplan life so that we never had to MacGyver anything. Some other camps had nice neat dining shelters, all safely self-contained but with, I think, less wildly beautiful a view than ours. Or maybe some campers plan everything so meticulously that they don't have to rely on stray corned beef hash tins, although somehow I doubt that. Much of camping seems to be a matter of MacGyvering. In fact, that's one of the things I liked best about camping. I like problem-solving, especially when it gets creative and maybe a little weird.

Our Enlightenment heritage teaches us to think of God as the Master Clockmaker: that God has A Plan, all worked out to the minutest detail—and yet that God-model simply does not fit with our experience. Or if it does, it makes a person wonder about a God who could preprogram (say) a beloved child's terminal cancer. . . . But what if God is doing with my life what I was doing with my camp? Getting a little creative? Taking an odder shortcut? Rigging it on the wing, at least a little? God's purpose, God's desired end, would stay constant, as the desired end of our MacGyvering was to have a sheltered place to eat that could handle the mountain rains. But maybe the means can get a little peculiar. "Necessity is the smother of intention," as someone once observed.

What if God is, in fact, adapting our course with us as we move through life, like a jazz player improvising on a chord chart? My camping trip brought me face to face with the past, and with past expectations that had, in fact, ended up being completely out of whack with the way my life had actually gone. I have done a lot of MacGyvering in my time, and it's fetched me up in interesting places. But they were not the places I could conceivably have planned for.

Only in retrospect can we see the patterns starting to emerge—how a guy line pulled tight here, a rope loosened there, an empty can of hash, can indeed make the structure we needed. Only by looking behind us at our lives can we see how God's MacGyvering can, in fact, build something that wasn't what we ever expected or could possibly have planned for, but which works. It's not looking into the future and worrying about it that helps us grow in faith; and certainly trying to control the future, to make it safe and predictable, is the very opposite of faith. Instead, we grow into faith by examining the trace of God in our experience, seeing how wonderfully well our Creator can MacGyver, if we give God the chance to get creative instead of trying to run the whole thing ourselves down to the last jot and tittle.

So do pack the tarp and the ropes and ties; don't forget some strong twine for guy lines. A good pole helps. But do trust that you'll figure out how it's all supposed to go together when you see what God has given you to work with. Call God creative. Even call God a sneaky son-of-a-something—I doubt if God minds. But God is at work, ends firmly in mind, taking us where it is God wants us to go—and that may be in directions where we never meant to go, but which fetch us up with more than we could ever ask or imagine.

Dead Tired

The cathedral was cool and dim after the flat-out sun and the noise of traffic in the city's center. There were a couple of middle-aged ladies there (they were very much ladies, too) as well as the friend I'd arranged to meet for noontime Communion. The priest, one of the archdeacons, was friendly, traditional, seemly, and sensible in a pleasantly dry way, rather like the building itself. We used the old Book of Common Prayer.

Life's been full of deep hard work lately, and as I listened to the Word proclaimed, I felt a wave of exhaustion possess me— ground-in tiredness, the sort that makes you feel as though you've been cut off at the knees. The gospel held out the image of birds sheltering in the branches of a mustard plant, grown from the smallest of seeds. What a fruitful tangle, full of places to hide and be safe! It was a comforting image. I could use a mustard bush right now. . . .

Because it was a noonday Eucharist, there was no collection, only the offering back to God of what God had given to us through creation. It occurred to me as the priest arranged the elements and started to make ready for the consecration: God wants us to give whatever it is we have most to share. That's what the offering is all about.

For some people, that might be money; if you've got it (and we almost all have *some* of it!) share it around. For some, it might be talents of one sort or another—music or needlework, gardening or writing, carpentry or cooking. For some, it might be the deep engagement of listening and working for and with others, love at its best. For some, it might be the service and discipline of the mind. Whatever.

For some, though, what we possess most of is sheer tiredness. Or pain or grief or anxiety or even anger—whatever it is we're most full of. We see these as burdens, not offerings, as things we offload with relief, not bring with pleasure. But who knows what God sees in them?

I don't for a moment doubt that when we offer God something whole and handsome and best-of-its-kind, God takes up the gift lovingly and with pleasure, as I accept any gift from my child with pleasure. But who says that God doesn't react the same way to our bringing these darker gifts, these gifts of imperfection? It's very human to want to sacrifice the creamy white heifer, virgin and unblemished, her horns sheathed in pure gold, because that's our human idea of a wonderful present to give God. But we've been told that that's not necessarily what God wants most. And our most perfectly beautiful gifts are, after all, still so very human and imperfect.

The willingness to let down and be tired with another person is a sign of intimacy, isn't it? It's a matter of trust, just as we can fumble and mumble and be unsure of ourselves, be human and needy, with the people we trust most. And we can do that because we trust their love to hold and sustain us when we need holding and sustenance.

So what does that say about what we can afford to bring to God? What *should* we be doing with God? Do we best love others by taking them into the front room and giving them formal tea from the good china, or by taking them into the kitchen and letting our hair down with them? Both are forms of love, and perhaps both are equal. One will do for you and the other for me. Neither is wrong. Both are love.

Of course it's right and proper and our bounden duty to bring the best of whatever we have to give to God. But it's important to remember that we do this for ourselves, not for God. We offer our best in order to stretch ourselves in loving ways, not to win God's favor, because that's setting Christ to one side and saying we don't need his sacrifice. We cannot earn God's love through doing it perfectly, following the rules, being at our best, because our best is wholly inadequate by God's standards. We can't come to the altar clean, dressed in our best, unstained and clear in conscience; it's just not on. Sometimes all we can do is to say, Okay, God, I'm here, I'm tired, I'm Yours.

It's a very human thing to say Joy is Good; Pain is Bad; I want to give God what is good, so I'll share joy and keep the pain to myself. But what God wants is *us*, in whatever condition we're in, happy or grousing, bubbly or worn right out, loving or awash in self-pity and grievances. Gifts are lovely; but what God's after is our selves, our souls and bodies—perfect or flabby, full of zeal and energy or falling-over tired.

Whatever you've got, give it. You don't know what price tag God puts on it, after all. It's probably safe to assume that God's values are not much like ours, and what seems unworthy to us may please God greatly. But don't worry about it. Just give whatever you have most of. It will do.

Grace Abounding

During the hard years all our gardens went: first, years ago, the big vegetable garden down in the field at the back; then the bed of hollyhocks by the stone wall; then the irises and daylilies alongside the garage; then the old perennial bed, out behind the garage—I dug out the best plants for the new perennial bed by the driveway—and finally the new perennial bed itself, where the peonies are still fighting it out with the wild violets, but the lupines went under without a trace.

I felt miserable about the waste and the ugliness, but I couldn't for the life of me manage, even after life turned around and started getting better. What with single motherhood, struggling with my own recovery and trying to make a living and run the household, dealing with all these gardens wasn't even an outside possibility. And I've never been much of a gardener. I get defeated easily, and I take no pleasure in weeding, as I do in cooking or even in folding laundry.

I tried now and again to tackle the mess, but it got uglier and bigger and deeper, especially when the wild brambles sprang up around the side and back of the garage. They were horrible to try to get rid of—tough, thorny, and tenacious, ready to spring back up if you left a thread of a root or the smallest tendrilly stem—and I already had more than enough to struggle with. So I just closed my eyes, metaphorically speaking, and let the wild things take over. I couldn't ever quite forget they were there, and I kept wondering what my nice next-door neighbors thought of the mess—but I did my best just to put it out of mind. If you can't fix it, it doesn't do any good to worry about it much.

Then, last Sunday afternoon, while we were out fixing the busted mailbox (bored local kids driving by with a baseball bat), the nice next-door neighbor lady said, "Did you know about those blackberries out back?" I just looked at her blankly. She said, "Around the side of the garage—you've got so many ripe berries, you'd better go get them before the birds do." So I went out around the back of the garage, which I haven't even looked at properly in maybe a couple-three years, and there it was: quite a splendid berry patch, bearing hugely, clusters of ripe berries wherever I looked.

I felt a little stunned: oh, such grace! Such abundance! Out of my mess and muddle, out of all this ugliness and angular mass of thorn, there comes such sweetness and freshness and fruitfulness. . . . If I'd been less of a rank failure as a gardener, these berries wouldn't be here. I got containers, and in under ten minutes we had maybe three quarts. Whole clusters of ripe berries, five or six at a time, tumbled into the palm of my hand at the lightest touch. There were so many left that I told the nice neighbors to help themselves, and there will still be lots left for the birds. And I have never tasted better berries in my life, perfectly balanced between the sweet and the tart and as full of flavor as a berry can be.

We ate our berries with very good vanilla ice cream (wonderful!). And then I got busy with other things, and my kid came down with the chickenpox, and I kept meaning to go out back and pick some more, but it's been One of Those Weeks. Until this morning, when the doorbell rang and my nice neighbor was there, with two jars of blackberry freezer jam. I'd given her free run of the patch, and she'd got busy, and here were the results. A couple of years ago, she had a run-in with breast cancer, and I put her on the prayer list and sent over some bread when she came home after the surgery, and it all meant more to her than I'd realized. This was her way of saying thank you.

We aren't normally close, but we hugged in my front hall, and I thought again: what mysteries can come of the mess we make of things, when we give the dear Lord permission to fool around.

I think I will bake some fresh bread on Sunday to put the jam on, and take a loaf over to my nice neighbors. And then I will have to learn how to keep this patch I've been so serendipitously given— although I am deeply grateful that it seems to do so well without my having much say in the matter. I am not a gardener, and I never will be. This is none of my doing; it is the grace of God and nature, redeeming the mess we make of things, working miracles without our even knowing it—out of our sight, in the bramble bushes we struggle through and with.

Evensong

Out for a walk on the loveliest of late summer evenings. The fields are still full of flowers—mostly Queen Anne's lace, but some thistles, clover, butter-and-eggs and other floral miscellanea, and the asters (my faves) are just now getting going. The air on my face was friendly, a little cool, a little damp—perfection. The peace of this quiet season, its mild reflectiveness, can get into a person, and that happened as I headed out along the path to the mall.

I ran my few errands, dawdling happily through the drugstore and supermarket, and started home with my backpack full of purchases—toothpaste and school supplies and a tub of cream cheese— just as the light was beginning to go. There was one particular moment when the light took on that odd quality it gets just before it starts to fade away: light that couples clarity with great gentleness.

It's not that anything's blurry in this light; in fact, things seem to stand out with greater definition, more precision—but without glare. There's nothing sharp about this light. It brings out the depths of color so that the red of a geranium seems more deeply joyous and the yellow of the butter-and-eggs flowers is strong and happy. There's no shift to the colors of things, merely an intensification of what they are, so that when you look at the grass you seem to be seeing the very soul of the color Green, and a neighbor's lobelia is the Perfection of Blue.

It occurred to me: if you want to know the truth of a thing, you need to bring it into bright light. There's nothing like bright light for showing you exactly what a thing looks like, all its bumps and hollows, its whiskers and wrinkles, or the fine details of its sags and slumps. My idea of hell is a brightly lit changing room in a clothing store. If this is truth, it definitely HURTS.

On the other hand, if you want to apprehend the mystery of a thing, you have to sidle up to its dark side—its contradictoriness, its unclarity, its hiddenness, what it will not reveal to you or what you cannot understand. Which is maybe why Christmas Eve is often so much more moving than Christmas Day.

But (maybe?) if you want to know the soul of a thing, you need to come looking for it when the light's like this—still bright enough for vision, but softened by a small side order of darkness. It's Truth with a smear of Mystery that gets at the heart of things.

If that's the case—and I'm only guessing here!—then maybe this is the sort of light that we face in God's face, at that moment when we stand before Him. He shows us what we have made for good or ill of the gifts of life and talents that He'd dowered us with. There is clarity in this vision; it doesn't hide or cover up anything. It will be a truthful accounting, and all that we thought we had successfully hidden will come into the light of day.

But that Light, while searching and truthful, will also be full of the mystery of Grace. It will reveal to us who we are, accurately and precisely. But I don't think it will be a halogen bulb blinding us and cruelly flattening out whatever beauty we have. I think it will show us what there is in ourselves to love, as well as to hang our heads about. I think it will be a light like this light, a light of gentleness and reflection as well as of clarity—a light that brings out our own rich colors, for us to see and understand.

We do well to leave God's incomprehensible grace at the core of belief, instead of trying to tease it out into something that isn't dark to us, for this reason: that the Light unsoftened by Mystery would be more than we could bear. When we extend that grace to another human being, instead of focusing on that person's failings, we do what we should hope and pray God will do for us—and if we don't think we need that grace, it's because we haven't looked at ourselves with any truthfulness at all.

If God clearly wants the dark gentleness of Mystery at the heart of things, who are we to argue?

The light slipped away that one small fraction, and then we were heading into true evening as the colors faded a little at a time and the sky darkened into lapis-lazuli deep blue. I found myself singing the last verse of a hymn I'd loved since childhood:

Lord of all gentleness, Lord of all calm,
Whose voice is contentment, whose presence is balm,
Be there at our sleeping, and give us, we pray,
Your peace in our hearts, Lord, at the end of the day.